COMPETITION AND COMPETITION POLICY

COMPETITION AND COMPETITION POLICY

A Comparative Analysis
of Central and
Eastern Europe

Edited by
Saul Estrin and Martin Cave

Pinter Publishers
London and New York

Distributed in the United States and Canada by St. Martin's Press

Pinter Publishers Ltd
25 Floral Street, Covent Garden, London, WC2E 9DS, United Kingdom

First published in 1993

© Editors and Contributors, 1993

Distributed exclusively in the USA and Canada by St. Martin's Press, Inc., Room 400, 175 Fifth Avenue, New York, NY 10010, USA

British Library Cataloguing in Publication Data
A CIP catalogue record for this book is available from the British Library

ISBN 1 85567 125 5

Library of Congress Cataloging-in-Publication Data
A CIP catalog record for this book is available from the Library of Congress

Typeset by Florencetype Ltd, Kewstoke, Avon
Printed and bound in Great Britain by Biddles Ltd, Guildford and King's Lynn

CONTENTS

LIST OF CONTRIBUTORS

Saul Estrin is Associate Professor of Economics at London Business School. Educated at Cambridge and Sussex Universities, he was previously Senior Lecturer at the London School of Economics. His research has concentrated on the socialist economies of Central and Eastern Europe, and he has written about planning, employee ownership and privatisation. He is currently acting as consultant to the World Bank on the economies in transition.

Martin Cave is Professor of Economics and Dean of the Faculty of Social Sciences at Brunel University. He has written articles and books in the field of economic planning, output measurement in the public sector and the economics of regulation. He has acted as Consultant to the UK Treasury, the Office of Fair Trading, OFTEL and other bodies.

Ferenc Vissi, born in 1946, is the President of the Office for Economic Competition in Hungary. He is a graduate of Budapest University of Economics. From 1973 he has been working in the state administration. He was one of the initiators of the present competition policy, and played an important role during the codification of the Competition Law. He has courses on competition policy at the Budapest University of Economics. Nearly 50 of his studies have been published in scientific reviews, journals or in books. He is a member of the Expert's Council of the Hungarian Economic Association.

Anna Fornalczyk, born in 1947, is a graduate of the Economics and Sociology Department of the University of Lodz, where she also earned a PhD in Economics. From 1968 to 1990 she worked at the University of Lodz, researching on organisational aspects of the centrally planned economy and the behaviour of enterprises in this economic system. The results of her researches were reported in two books and many articles and papers. In April 1990 she was appointed the President of the Antimonopoly Office; the first competition agency in the post-communist countries. From that time she has been responsible for enforcement of competition law in Poland.

Lina Takla was first employed as a researcher at the Centre for Economic Performance in the Post-Communist Reform Programme, and subsequently as Research Officer for the Centre for Business Strategy at the London Business School. She has recently been appointed Research Fellow in International Economics at the Royal Institute of International Affairs, responsible for Eastern European issues. She is also a consultant to the World Bank on Czech enterprise adjustment. Her current research analyses enterprise behaviour in transition, privatisation, competition policy and industrial structure in Czechoslovakia.

Paul Hare has been Professor of Economics at Heriot-Watt University since 1985, and a part-time senior researcher at LSE's Centre for Economic Performance since 1990. He also directs Heriot-Watts University's Centre for Economic Reform and Transformation, which carries out research on the central and eastern European economies in transition. Professor Hare has written numerous books and articles on aspects of economic development in eastern Europe, most recently writing on industrial competitiveness and privatisation.

Jan Korenovsky has been since 1990 the Chairman of the Slovak Anti-Monopoly Department, one of the three competition policy offices in what used to be the Czech and Slovak Federal Republic. Since the country divided in January 1993, the department has become the competition policy office of the newly independent Slovak republic. Dr Eugen Jurzyca also works for the same department.

Eugen Jurzyca works at the Antimonopoly Office of the Slovak Republic (AOSR) as a Third Executive Department Deputy Director. Within AOSR he is in charge of investigation of cartel contracts, mergers, abuses of market power as well as with public procurement policy, regulation of natural monopolies and privatisation process. He was involved in preparation of the government decree on public procurement and the coordinator of the group responsible for preparation of the Act on Regulation of Natural Monopolies. From 1981 to 1990 he worked for the agency responsible for price-setting rules of building pieces within the Czechoslovak republic. Simultaneously he works as a tutor for City University Bratislava (the branch of Open University). His specialisation here is marketing. He participated at the Pew Economic Freedom Fellows Program from January 1993 to June 1993. This program combines intensive academic coursework, structured practicums, and first-hand observation of American government and industry for twenty emerging economic policy-makers from countries undergoing rapid democratisation and transformation to free market systems. He is a graduate of the University of Economics in Bratislava, Slovakia.

Mark Schaffer is a Research Fellow at the Centre for Economic Performance, London School of Economics. He was previously a lecturer in economics at University of Sussex. He was educated at Harvard (BA),

Stanford (MA) and the London School of Economics (MSc and PhD in economics). He is an expert on the economies of Central and Eastern Europe. His current research is on the business sector in transition economies.

Philippe Aghion was formerly deputy chief economist at the European Bank for Reconstruction and Development. He continues to be associated with the bank but is now a fellow of Nuffield College, Oxford.

Kurt Stockmann studied law at Berlin and Freiburg Universitite, and practised as an attorney during the 1960s. He joined the German Federal Cartel Office in 1971, and has been Chairman of the Decisions Divisions since 1984. He is also Chairman of the OECD Committee on Competition Law and Policy.

Jean-Patrice de la Laurencie. Before joining Coudert Frères, Jean-Patrice de La Laurencie held a number of posts within the French Ministry of Finance between 1971 and 1989, including financial adviser in the French Representation to the European Communities (1975–77) and adviser in the Ministry of Finance's Cabinet (Mr Delors 1981–82), and most recently as Deputy Director General of the Finance Ministry's Competition, Consumer Affairs and Anti-Fraud Department. In this last position, he participated actively in the drafting of the French antitrust legislation and in the elaboration of the EC merger control regulation.

Sally J Van Siclen received an AB from Duke University in 1980 in economics and mathematics, an MA from Princeton University in 1985 and a PhD in economics from Princeton University in 1987. From 1986 until 1992 she was an economist in the Economic Analysis Group of the Antitrust Division of the US Department of Justice. Since June 1992 she has been an administrator in the Competition and Consumer Policy Division of the Organisation for Economic Cooperation and Development. Her responsibilities there include coordinating and providing competition policy advice to countries in transition to market economies.

PREFACE

In 1990 the Economic and Social Research Council (ESRC) responded to the economic, political and social transformation taking place in Eastern Europe and the (then) USSR by establishing a special initiative – the East-West Initiative – to examine the course of events as they unfold, to apply appropriate social science techniques to the economies and societies in transition and to draw out the appropriate conclusions for the ESRC's audience in the research, business and policy-making communities.

Twenty-one projects have now been selected as part of the Initiative, covering the following areas: transition to the market economy; labour relations; democratisation; constitutional reforms; social consequences. A further set of projects concerns attitudinal surveys in the region. The projects are linked together by a Co-ordinator and the Initiative as a whole is closely associated with similar work carried out in Western Europe and the United States. In addition, many of the projects involve participation from social scientists in the countries under study.

This volume contains contributions to a conference organised by one of the teams involved in the Initiative. Its contents reflect many of the aims of the Initiative: the adoption of a comparative approach, the application of Western theoretical and policy perspectives, the participation of policy-makers from the economies in transition, and a focus on an issue of considerable importance, both in the short and the long term. It is one of what will be a substantial number of publications from the Initiative.

Howard Newby
Chairman, ESRC

FOREWORD

This volume has been published as a result of the reactions to a Conference held at the London Business School on 7 and 8 June 1992 on 'Competition Policy and the Regulation of Utilities During Transition'. We had been working for more than a year on this subject as part of our research project, funded by the ESRC East-West Initiative, 'Transition to a Market Economy: Competitiveness, Ownership and Regulation'. The idea behind the Conference was to stimulate discussion between practitioners from both economies in transition and developed Western market economies about the conduct of competition policy, with interventions from interested academics, consultants and representatives of Western businesses.

The Conference exceeded our expectations in the calibre of the contributions and discussions and in the interest which was stimulated. This encouraged us to produce a book on the competition policy aspects of transition only (the material on regulation was less developed at that point), based on the original Conference contributions, with some invited additional papers to round off the argument as well as an introduction to set the scene, and conclusions from the study as a whole.

We would like gratefully to acknowledge financial support from the ESRC East-West Initiative and the Centre for Business Strategy. Nicola Viinikka from Pinter Publishers has been a supportive editor and neither the Conference nor the book could have been finalised without the unceasing efforts of Eleanor Burke. We have benefited from discussions about these issues with other members of the research group – Judy Batt, Paul Hare and Lina Takla – and from our colleagues at LSE, LBS and Brunel University. We are grateful also to Dr. Martin Howe of the Office of Fair Trading and Professor David Stout of the Centre for Business Strategy for chairing the conference sessions. Any remaining errors of fact and understanding are however entirely our own.

Saul Estrin, London Business School and London School of Economics
Martin Cave, Brunel University
November 1992

1 INTRODUCTION

Martin Cave and Saul Estrin

The economic transformation now occurring in Central Eastern Europe involves numerous dimensions. The most conspicuous relate to macro-economic stabilisation and to transfers of ownership from the public to the private sector. But perhaps equally fundamental, if less discussed, is the wholesale reconstruction of the resource allocation mechanism taking place in many of the economies, whatever their macro-economic state and however productive assets are owned. This switch from a 'command' to a 'market' system of resource allocation, which is associated with price and trade liberalisation and the establishment of a Western-type commercial code, places enormous demands upon the accounting, legal and regulatory structures of the countries in transition.

Thus countries in Central and Eastern Europe are forced to replace bookkeeping systems largely used for the purposes of central control by accounting systems more appropriate for a market economy. A whole framework of business and commercial law including bankruptcy regulations has to be created almost from scratch, to cope with situations in which production units contract freely with one another, rather than respond to central orders. New regulatory systems have to be introduced to combat abuses, including fraud and abuse of market power.

This volume is concerned with one element of this system: the development of competition policy. Since competition, however, cannot be considered independently from initial market structures and potential import penetration, other elements of micro-economic relevance cannot be ignored. We focus particularly upon what has been happening in the Czech and Slovak Federal Republic (CSFR), Hungary and Poland which are the most advanced as yet in this area, although references are also made to developments in other economies in transition, including Russia. The contributors include Western academic experts on competition policy, practitioners of competition law and policy in Western Europe and – most importantly – individuals from the CSFR, Hungary and Poland currently engaged in the difficult task of developing and applying competition policy in their own countries. A major theme will concern what can be learnt from Western experience, and what is special about competition policy in transforming economies.

The aim of this introduction is to provide background information relating to the theory of competition policy and competition law and policy as it is applied in Western Europe and the United States. This is followed by an account of features of the economies in transition which are particularly relevant to the development of competition policy in these countries, and a summary of current competition legislation in the CSFR, Hungary and Poland. We do not aim to draw any firm conclusions here, but to provide the necessary background information against which the more detailed contributions which follow can be set.

1. The theory of competition policy

The traditional starting-point for discussions of competition policy in Western economic analysis is the bench-mark provided by the model of perfectly competitive markets. If a market is competitive in the sense that it contains a large number of firms, that each firm takes the price as given and entry and exit are cheap, then it can be shown that the resulting market equilibrium will be characterised by productive efficiency. Competition among firms will ensure that only the most efficient will survive and prices will reflect marginal costs. Moreover, if all markets are perfectly competitive, then those prices will be such as to sustain allocative efficiency: i.e. consumers (if they are well informed and rational) will be guided by them to choose combinations of goods which optimally meet their preferences.

The perfectly competitive model, with its associated optimality properties, is no more than a bench-mark. In reality, markets which are less rigorously competitive – sometimes known as 'workably competitive' – are often regarded as satisfactory, in the sense that they do not require policy intervention. In other cases, markets may be potentially competitive or contestable, even though they contain few firms, and may be considered not to merit intervention. But not all markets will satisfy even these looser conditions. Some will be sufficiently concentrated or monopolised for price to deviate substantially and persistently from marginal cost, thus distorting the structure of consumption, preventing the attainment of productive and allocative efficiency and giving the firm's owners excess profits. The theory of competition policy is concerned with identifying cases where these departures from optimality are sufficient to justify intervention and with establishing the appropriate instruments to intervene. Monopolies – loosely described as markets in which one firm or a group of firms acting together establish a dominant position – most clearly illustrate a departure from a competitive outcome and suggest the implied remedies. If the monopoly is making excess profits or is inefficient, then the obvious remedies are either to break it up to restore the competitive outcome or to regulate prices, at the same time seeking to promote efficiency. The latter solution is typically applied in industries which are perceived as being 'natural monopolies' – i.e. industries where economies of scale and scope are so large that production is carried on most cheaply by a single firm. Such industries are typically public utilities relying on networks of wires and pipes to distribute their products, and in most Western countries special arrangements are made to regulate them, normally through price controls. But we are concerned in this volume primarily with industries which are not natural monopolies and where introducing a degree of competition rather than regulation is the appropriate policy. In such cases, breaking up the monopoly is an attractive approach to the abuse of monopoly power.

The second main area of application of competition policy concerns anti-competitive practices used by a firm in order to gain or maintain a position of dominance in a market. This is a more controversial area in the theory of competition policy, as disputes exist about which practices adversely affect consumers' welfare.

Most economists agree that explicit horizontal agreements among firms in the same market to fix prices or prohibit entry are detrimental to consumers. If firms are able to form 'cartels' in this way, they can raise prices as high as those which would be charged by a monopolist without any compensating advantages in the form of economies of scale or rationalised production. They are thus highly unlikely to promote efficiency, and in most jurisdictions they are prohibited, or allowed only in exceptional cases. Agreements by firms to share R & D costs create a more difficult dilemma because of the public good aspects of scientific knowledge. For this reason, co-operation in basic or strategic research is sometimes permitted, even though agreements to share near-market research and development costs are often prohibited.

The second and more controversial type of potentially anti-competitive practices involves vertical agreements or constraints – i.e. agreements between a supplier and customer. The main practices included in this heading are as follows:

Retail price maintenance: the manufacturer imposes upon the retailer a minimum price at which a product can be sold.

Exclusive dealing: a retailer undertakes to sell only one manufacturer's product, and not the output of rival firms.

Territorial exclusivity: a particular retailer is given sole rights to sell the products of a manufacturer in a specified area.

Quantity discounts: retailers receive progressively larger discounts the more of a given manufacturer's product they sell – this obviously gives them an incentive at the margin to push one manufacturer's product at the expense of another's.

Tie-in sales: restraints which require the retailer to take good X if he or she is to be supplied with good Y – by this means, a manufacturer can extend a monopoly in one market into another, and discourage new entry (by forcing a prospective entrant to come into both markets simultaneously).

Long-term supply contracts: these bind a retailer to a supplier and often can only be terminated by the retailer at great cost.

At first sight many of these practices look anti-competitive, in the sense that they either prohibit retailers from discounting products or prevent other retailers from entering the market. The problem, however, is that almost all of them are capable of economic justification as being potentially to the benefit of consumers, and fashions in economics have fluctuated substantially between condemnation of them and acceptance of them as being in the public interest.

We can illustrate the dilemma by considering the arguments for and against territorial exclusivity. On the one hand, it seems profoundly anti-competitive to allow the manufacturer to license a particular retailer to hold a monopoly of distribution in an area. By restricting the power of other retailers to enter the market, the effect may be to raise prices and to damage consumers' interests. On the other hand, territorial exclusivity may operate in consumers' interest in certain cases. Let us take the case of a product which consumers need to examine and test before they buy it. If several retailers are allowed to sell the product in a particular area, each will try to encourage potential buyers to inspect and test the product in other stores and buy it at a discount in their own. Thus no retailer will have an incentive to provide proper inspection or related facilities, but will try to 'free-ride' on other retailers. As a consequence, consumers in the end will have no facilities to make a proper inspection of the product they intend to buy. With the system of territorial exclusivity, each retailer will have a local monopoly and thus have no opportunity to free-ride on others' facilities. Hence this particular form of vertical restraint may operate in the customers' interest. Similar arguments can be constructed for or against other forms of constraint listed above, although it has proved much harder to produce a convincing argument in favour of retail price maintenance (RPM) which is generally prohibited in the UK and in certain other countries.

A third form of anti-competitive practice is predatory pricing, normally defined as an attempt by a firm (or group of firms) to lower its price, drive a competitor out of the market, and then raise prices again. Controversy over predatory pricing has centred upon two issues. The first is whether it is rational for a profit-maximising firm to engage in it. The argument here is that if a firm is threatened by many potential entrants, a policy of predatory pricing may be costly, as it will have to drive out not one but many competitors. It is possible to construct models in which predatory pricing is rational, but there is still considerable debate about whether it is likely to occur in practice.

The second complexity relating to predatory pricing concerns the definition of when it is occurring. Predatory pricing is pricing below cost, but what is the appropriate cost yardstick? Possible candidates put forward include short-run marginal cost, long-run marginal cost, average variable cost and incremental cost. Theoretical or practical cases can be made for several of these, and the issue is clearly important in determining whether predation has or has not occurred.

This brief account has demonstrated that while the theory of competition policy for market economies is straightforward, its application to real market problems is controversial. It is thus hardly surprising that different Western countries have adopted divergent approaches to competition. We describe these briefly in the next section, as an indication of what Western precedents are available for economies in transition.

2. Western models of competition policy

Economies in transition have naturally sought 'off the shelf' solutions to the problems of constructing an appropriate institutional, legal and regulatory framework within which their markets will operate. Given the pace of change, it is natural that they should seek to resolve the issues in this way. It is also noteworthy that they have received a considerable amount of advice, solicited or unsolicited, from Western experts or practitioners in competition law.

Decisions about what models to adopt are to a large degree predetermined by the country's international economic policy. This phenomenon finds its most obvious expression in the desire on the part of most economies in transition to seek membership or association with the European Community. Adherence to the Treaty of Rome will ultimately make the country concerned subject to Articles 85 and 86, and to the Community's arrangements for merger approvals. The expectation of membership thus imposes some restrictions on the form of competition law chosen, although the EC presently contains countries with widely divergent national competition laws.

The most advanced countries on the transition path have less leeway; the Articles of Association signed between the EC and the CSFR, Hungary and Poland on 22 November 1991 contain for the first time an explicit discussion of Competition Policy. Article 63 of these 'Europe Agreements' made cartel agreements, abuse by firms of dominant positions in the EC and associated state markets and any public accord which either acts or threatens to disrupt competition incompatible with the functioning of the agreement. The criteria for assessing these provisons are Articles 85, 86 and 92 of the Treaty of Rome. Moreover, the 'Europe Agreements' lay out a timetable for adoption of these provisions by 1 January 1995 (except for the provisions on state aids, which must be in place by 1 January 1997).

For the purposes of this introduction, it is sufficient to set out the range of competition law used in Western countries in a schematic way. As some of the contributions later in this volume show, the detailed wording of any country's legislation is often crucial to the resolution of particular cases. None the less, it is sufficient in our terms to describe the range of possible options in more general terms. (For more details see Boner and Krueger, 1991 and Fox, 1986.)

At the institutional level, Western countries differ in the role which judicial decisions play in defining and enforcing competition law. The dominant practice, followed by Germany and the USA (which have served as models for anti-trust legislation in most of the rest of the world) and shared with Australia, Japan, Canada, the EC and France, is for judicial decisions to play a central role. The alternative tradition, which employs an administrative system for the interpretation of the law with appointments to the administrative body made by a member of the Executive Branch, is exhibited by the UK, Spain and Sweden. Decisions whether to go down the judicial or the administrative route have an important impact on the costs and style of working of the competition authorities. The administrative approach promotes more informal procedures, but is widely considered to be less appropriate if penalties are to be levied for infringement of competition law.

A more fundamental conceptual distinction is between systems of competition law which focus upon dominance, and those which focus upon market power. Market power depends upon the relative size, or market share of firms, as well as upon other considerations such as entry barriers, the availability of substitutes, etc. Dominance, on the other hand, depends upon the absolute size of the supplier and its ability to determine outcomes for its trading partners. Competition law with an emphasis on market power normally starts from recognition of the link between competition and efficiency. It is thus primarily concerned with the extension of competition, on the hypothesis that consumers will thereby benefit. Competition law founded on dominance is usually more directly focused upon protection of consumers as an aim to be achieved directly, rather than indirectly through the promotion of competition. While US law focuses on competition, many European countries and the EC place more weight on dominance.

Competition law permits intervention in three principal areas: in the structure of economic markets, in the conduct of business and in economic performance. Structural regulation essentially takes the form of policy towards monopolies and mergers. An industry's structure can be altered by breaking up a monopolist, or preserved by preventing a merger. Naturally, one of the key issues here is determination of the size of the market in which an alleged monopoly is said to exist or be threatened. Depending upon their industrial policy tradition and openness to trade, countries differ in the degree to which they regard a national monopoly as beneficial or detrimental. Thus some governments promote 'national champions' in particular sectors, arguing that size in relation to the domestic market is an essential prerequisite for effective performance internationally. Others apply a narrower definition of markets and adopt harsher policies on domestic markets which are highly concentrated. Such distinctions are clearly also related to the absolute size of economies. 'Small' economies typically trade a proportionately larger share of output than large ones, as for instance Belgium compared with the United States. It might therefore be argued that competition policy is of less significance in 'smaller' countries. This kind of reasoning has ramifications for comparing, say, Hungary with Russia.

The general trend of structural regulation in Western countries has been in the direction of tightening it against monopolistic structures. Notably, since September 1990 new merger control regulations have given the European Commission responsibility for regulation of big 'mergers'. In some cases the Commission has taken over from national competition authorities, but some of the countries of the EC have no merger controls, so that the new development tightened control over industrial structure in Europe.

In the case of conduct regulation, countries differ in the extent to which they regard practices outlined in the previous section as being anti-competitive. In some jurisdictions, for example the United States, some practices are regarded as being illegal *per se*: i.e. no counterveiling benefit can justify the practice. Others are evaluated on a 'rule of reason' basis: i.e. a cost benefit test is applied, and if the benefits exceed the costs, the practice is not prohibited. The United States, Germany and the EC establish a stricter standard for justifying practices which may constrain competition than do other countries such as Sweden and the United Kingdom. In the latter, restraints may be judged on the basis of other criteria, although the relative weights given to these considerations have differed from period to period.

Finally, performance regulation involves direct control of companies' price or output decisions by the competition authority. This kind of remedy is permissible in many countries, but it is rarely used as part of standard competition law. We noted earlier its widespread use in relation to utilities which are often seen as being natural monopolies, but such regulation is normally undertaken by a specific regulatory body separate from the country's principal competition authorities.

A final important dimension concerns the nature of the enforcement process. Most European countries rely predominantly upon public enforcement: this involves an investigation or trial conducted by the competition authority, leading to an appropriate remedy – which may be an instruction to desist, a fine or some other conclusion. The alternative approach is private enforcement. This involves an injured party conducting a civil action against the alleged injurer, which may be required to pay damages to the plaintiff if the suit is successful. In the United States, such action is encouraged by the operation in certain circumstances of a 'triple damages' rule, according to which the damages paid are calculated as three times the injury which the plaintiff is found to have suffered. Private enforcement is a powerful means of enlisting the incentives of victims of monopolistic or anti-competitive behaviour to eliminate it. There are, however, possible disadvantages. In particular, the prospect of triple damages may encourage wasteful suits brought on the basis of a very low expectation of high reward. For this or other reasons, private enforcement is rarely used in Europe.

We have thus identified a set of dimensions in which Western countries differ in their application of competition law. These implicitly define the range of tried and tested options available to economies in transition. We now turn to examine the special economic circumstances which those countries face.

3. Features of the economies in transition relevant to competition policy

3.1 Ownership structures

The most obvious, and possibly the most important, difference between economies in transition and the stable market economies whose competition law has been described in the previous section is in ownership of resources. Although privatisation has recently affected the balance between public and private ownership in some economies in transition somewhat, the latter inherit state sectors which represent a proportion of national output far above the proportion found in Western economies containing the highest levels of public ownership. An indication of the scale of the differences is given in Table 1.1. This shows, for example, that in 1986, 97 per cent of output in Czechoslovakia was accounted for by the state sector, while the equivalent proportion in the United States three years earlier was 1.3 per cent.

The difference in ownership structure has several important implications for the development of competition policy in economies in transition:

a. if policy is to be effective in the short and medium term it will have to cover the state-owned as well as the private sector. Given the relatively slow pace of privatisation to date in many countries in transition, it seems likely that the state-owned sector will continue to be sizeable for a number of years. If competition policy is to work, it must be brought to bear on state-owned firms as well as upon privately owned firms;

b. competition policy will be applied during the period of changing property rights and ownership structures. This will create particularly sharp conflicts with the state. In particular, the desire to maximise privatisation revenues or to make enterprise available and thus meet privatisation targets may encourage governments to protect firms from increased competition. Some examples of this phenomenon can already be observed (Langenfeld and Blitzer, 1991, pp 384);

c. where restructuring is occurring as well as changing property rights, there risks being a lack of clarity in establishing who is responsible for anti-competitive acts.

3.2 Market structures

The industrial structures of the economies in transition were developed to suit the preferences of socialist planners rather than to provide competitive markets. In one sense the economy was organised as a giant firm with the basic structure of output and inter-firm transactions being decided by planners at the centre, and instructions then being transmitted through a bureaucratic hierarchy based upon industrial ministries. Production units operated formally on an 'independent accounting' (*khoz-*

Table 1.1 The share of the state sector in European countries

		Percent of Output	Percent of Employment
Eastern Europe			
Czechoslovakia	(1986)	97.0	–
East Germany	(1982)	96.5	94.2
Soviet Union	(1985)	96.0	–
Poland	(1985)	81.7	71.5
China	(1984)	73.6	–
Hungary	(1984)	65.2	69.9
Western Europe[*]			
France	(1982)	16.5	14.6
Austria	(1978/9)	14.5	13.0
Italy	(1982)	14.0	15.0
Turkey	(1985)	12.2	20.0
Sweden		–	10.6
Finland		–	10.0
United Kingdom	(1978)	11.1	8.2
West Germany	(1982)	10.7	7.8
Portugal	(1976)	9.7	–
Denmark	(1974)	6.3	5.0
Greece	(1979)	6.1	–
Norway		–	6.0
Spain	(1979)	4.1	–
Netherlands	(1971/3)	3.6	8.0
United States	(1983)	1.3	1.8

Source: Milanovic (1989), Tables 1.4 and 1.7
[*] Excludes government services, but includes state-owned enterprises engaged in commercial activities.

raschet) basis, but the planners repeatedly changed the boundaries of enterprises. They frequently reduced the number of firms through amalgamation in order to facilitate the planning process. As a consequence, both 'enterprises' and plants were very large by Western standards. For example, the average number of workers in each enterprise in Central Europe was several times larger than in the OECD. This enterprise giganticism was also a consequence of planners' concentration on the supply of intermediate products and on heavy industry, where economies of scale are considerable.

It is widely believed that a concentrated market structure has deleterious effects upon competition. This matter has been widely investigated for Western economies, but there are few studies covering Eastern Europe. One of the few sources that is available is Estrin (1983), who studied industrial structure in Yugoslavia in the 1950s and 1960s after the first reforms to the central planning systems. Estrin found that:

a. the economy had very few firms – only about 2,500 in the manufacturing sector. Small and medium-sized firms were virtually completely absent. (In contrast, 70 per cent of US and 50 per cent of UK enterprises employ less than 30 people. The absence of small firms has also been widely noted by observers of the current situation in Hungary, Poland and particularly the CSFR, where the private sector has been slow to develop in comparison. It is intended that reforms will everywhere change the situation by encouraging the rapid development of the small-scale private sector, and some progress is being made in this respect. But many of the firms created quickly fail, because of the tight monetary and fiscal policy associated with macro-stabilisation.);
b. as a consequence, the number of firms operating in Yugoslav markets was small. In 1959, some 18 per cent of Yugoslav industries contained 10 firms or fewer, and around 66 per cent had 25 firms or less. Only in 5 per cent of industries were there more than 100 producers. Industrial concentration rates were correspondingly very high. In the case of product supply, the situation was even worse. When disaggregation was taken down to the level of specific product markets, 15 per cent of them in 1959 were found to have been served by only one firm, with a further 12 per cent of product markets having two suppliers only.

These Yugoslav data, though old, provide an illustration of the very high levels of market concentration economies in transition are likely to exhibit. More recent data for Poland (see Table 1.2) show the number of firms accounting for 50 per cent or 80 per cent of total Polish manufacturing output. It can be seen that:

a. the total number of firms is very small by Western standards – just over 5,000, compared with over 100,000 industrial enterprises in the UK and more than 300,000 in the United States;
b. even at the relatively high aggregation represented by the Table, the number of firms in each sector is quite small: nine of the 22 sectors have fewer than 100 enterprises, 6 fewer than 50;
c. industrial concentration is also very high: in more than one-third of the sectors fewer than one-third of firms account for half the output or more, and in four sectors, fewer than 10 firms account for 80 per cent of the output. Conversely, only in six sectors do more than 100 firms account for 80 per cent of output. The figures themselves understate actual market power because there are many different markets within most of the sectors (e.g. chemicals or engineering) and because in a large country like Poland many firms will supply a regional rather than a national market. Given the highly concentrated market structure, the natural remedy is to break up enterprises in order to promote competition. But difficulties often stand in the way of this approach. Although some enterprises consist of several plants which can readily be restructured, in many cases all or a very high proportion of output is accounted for by a single plant. In such circumstances restructuring may be impossible.

Table 1.2 Market structure in Poland, 1989

	Total No. of Enterprises	Total No. of Enterprises which account for	
		50%	80%
		of total output	
TOTAL	5,136	175	909
Group I – 8 Industries Employment – 30.3%			
Fuels	23	1	7
Non-ferrous Metallurgy	12	1	3
Ferrous Metallurgy	43	2	10
Coal	15	2	4
Feedstock	22	4	8
Paper	63	5	16
Ceramics	31	5	13
Transport Engineering	253	7	28
Group II – 4 Industries Employment – 9.2%			
Precise Engineering	137	10	32
Energy	70	11	31
Glass	81	11	27
Leather	211	13	46
Group III – 4 Industries Employment – 19.6%			
Printing	124	20	51
Electrical Engineering	283	20	63
Metal Working	477	26	95
Chemicals	389	26	80
Group IV – 4 Industries Employment – 28.2%			
Building Materials	319	30	101
Mechanical Engineering	520	33	135
Foodstuffs	769	38	196
Wood Working	417	39	104
Group V – 2 Industries Employment – 12.6%			
Ready-made Cloth	486	52	193
Textile	391	57	132

Source: Przemysl, 1990; GUS, Warszawa 1991

3.3 Vertical integration

Another widely noted feature of centrally planned economies was the high degree of vertical integration they exhibited. Planned economies were typically run in a taut way: output targets were taut and inputs supplied were not always adequate to meet the output targets. The supply system was also poorly co-ordinated, with surpluses developing in some enterprises co-existing with deficits in others, and only a rather inadequate unofficial 'market' available to redistribute them. Moreover, the complexity of the planning process often required the centre to close the plan at a time when it was internally inconsistent in the input-output sense. Thus even if resources were optimally distributed they might still have been inadequate to meet the output targets. As a consequence, managers had strong incentives to build up their own productive capacity for certain key inputs. For example, factories built their own foundries, machine shops and retail and distribution centres. In order to attract labour, which was typically scarce, they also provided health, child care and holiday facilities for their work-forces.

As we discussed in the first section, the implications of vertical integration for competition are complex. On one hand, the practices described above may reduce market concentration by encouraging a rather special form of 'entry'. On the other hand, vertical integration might give an enterprise market power. For example, possession of housing stock or control over leisure or retail facilities in the area could be used as an entry precluding device.

3.4 Relative prices

An important implication of the directive nature of the centrally planned economies is that prices played little part in the allocation system and were used principally as accounting and aggregating devices. In consequence, they failed to reflect scarcities, either within the country, within the trading bloc (the CMEA) or within the world trading system. One of the principal aberrations was dramatic underpricing of raw materials such as energy. As an illustration, when Poland increased its oil price by 600 per cent in January 1990 it still reached only one-third of the world level. Capital inputs were also either costless or available at very low cost, although they were invariably rationed. As a consequence, many industries in economies in transition exhibit very low, or even negative, value added at world prices, as shown in Hare and Hughes (1992).

As economies in transition are brought into the world trading system, their distorted prices will have to be discarded. This process will have significant implications for competition policy because:

a. the transition will be associated with dramatic changes in both relative and absolute prices. It will thus be hard to use price observations to draw conclusions about the presence or absence of anti-competitive conduct, for example, predatory pricing, or monopolistic pricing;

b. enterprises will be generally ignorant of costs, and will need to learn about the relation between costs and prices in the new system. This may lead to innocent 'mistakes', as well as the pursuit of anti-competitive objectives or price gouging. The high level of 'noise' in the system will inevitably make it harder for even a committed competition policy agency to identify categorically monopolistic and anti-competitive practices.

3.5 *Trade restrictions*

Planned economies traditionally had planned trade, a disproportionate amount of which took place within the Council for Mutual Economic Assistance (CMEA), the Eastern trading bloc. Trade with the West was limited, and in the unreformed economies trading decisions were taken by a monopoly Ministry of Foreign Trade. Exchange rates were not convertible, imports were rationed centrally together with all other inputs and exports were a component in the overall output plan targets. Although Hungary and Poland in particular moved towards more and freer trade with the West before the overthrow of the communist regimes, all the countries lacked currency convertibility.

Thus despite the fact that the CSFR, Hungary and Poland are all relatively small and open economies, they were largely insulated from international competition, especially from their Western neighbours. In order to make competition through trade effective it is necessary to introduce currency convertibility and to eradicate import licences and quotas, replacing them, if necessary, by tariffs.

To some extent reforms along these lines have been enacted in the three countries. Poland is the most advanced, with internal current account convertibility, the virtual elimination of import controls and extremely low tariffs. But Hungary and Czechoslovakia have also made considerable strides in the same direction.

It is generally agreed, however, that trade liberalisation is probably better viewed as an aid to domestic competition rather than as a substitute for it. Undervalued exchange rates may protect domestic producers, a situation which has many macro-economic advantages for economies in transition, and in any case not all goods and services are traded. In particular, international competition may be unequal or non-existent in many areas which require fuller development in the economies in transition, such as housing, health care, retail distribution and services.

3.6 *The rule of law*

We noted above that the process of transition often required the development of completely new institutional, legal and regulatory frameworks. Whereas market economies base their economic relations on the rule of law, in the sense that transactions are made on the basis of voluntary exchange, set out in contracts which are enforceable through the courts, in centrally planned economies, economic decisions were based upon orders transmitted from higher levels in a bureaucratic hierarchy. In traditional enterprise laws in centrally planned economies, activities were forbidden unless they were specifically authorised – in contrast to commercial law in market economies which is normally formulated in negative terms.

The situation was complicated further by the presence in centrally planned economies of an informal hierarchy, based upon the Party, which in practice was more powerful than the formal hierarchy based upon the government or the courts. Independence of the judiciary was a sham, disguising totalitarian control by the Party.

The lack of a tradition of a rule of law places exceptional burdens on the development of competition law and policy during the transition. In particular, it may be preferable to enforce and administer competition law through administrative bodies rather than a judiciary which in the past has earned no public respect. The lack of a tradition of commercial law may also militate in favour of rules which are simple and general, rather than requiring complex analysis and justification. However, other considerations enter into this choice as well.

3.7 Absence of capital markets

Traditional centrally planned economies lacked any semblance of capital markets. The banking system consisted typically of a single monopoly central bank, whose main function within the enterprise sector was to record the money value of inter-enterprise transactions which were determined by the plan. Retail banking was undeveloped. The only financial assets were cash and bank deposits, and the only liabilities were overdrafts. Despite limited (and sometimes compulsory) sales of debt to the population, the governments largely financed their activities by printing money.

Reforms in Hungary after 1968 and in Poland after 1981 did encourage the emergence of a commercial banking sector but the development of Western type capital markets was restricted by:

a. low domestic savings;
b. scarcity of personnel to work in capital market institutions and lack of expertise in the evaluation of risk or the management of portfolios;
c. shortage of individuals willing to undertake risks;
d. the limited development of financial instruments;
e. lack of competition in the banking sector;
f. the weak and deteriorating portfolios of existing financial institutions, whose assets consisted largely in loans made to finance often unprofitable projects in the enterprise sector.

The significance of this for competition policy is obvious. Weakness of domestic capital markets creates a major barrier to entry. Incumbents can charge high prices and operate inefficiently without a threat of domestically financed competitors.

The lack of domestic savings and domestic financial institutions increases the potential importance of foreign direct investment. Despite growing recourse to foreign capital through government loans, before the collapse of communism the three countries imposed major restrictions on foreign ownership of firms, in many cases limiting participation to a minority stake and restricting the repatriation of property. The current situation in the CSFR, Hungary and Poland has changed enormously from that, as can be seen in Table 1.3. Foreign direct investment is therefore an important potential source of funds. However, foreign investors are, not surprisingly, often eager to make their investment conditional upon monopolistic concessions. They are also only too aware of the precarious position of many of the economies in transition.

Thus in the longer term, development of domestic financial institutions is important for the growth of competition. Precisely what form these should take – the Anglo-American form of hands-off investment by institutions and individuals or the continental form of long-term relationships between banks and companies – is a matter for separate debate.

3.8 Habits of collusion

Finally, managers in centrally planned economies have traditionally been trained to regard themselves as cogs in larger organisations, even though they were often obliged to practise concealment or deception of their superiors over such matters as plan fulfilment. Habits of co-operation with colleagues (for example trading inputs with other enterprises) were ingrained. These practices have persisted through the transition period.

The introduction of competition requires the dissolution of traditional collusive practices. Existing managers must learn to compete, or new managers must take their place. The process of reform is thus likely to be advanced by transfers of ownership which lead to the appointment of more entrepreneurial and competitive managers.

This list of impediments to the development of competition policy shows the very severe handicaps to which the economies in transition are subject. In the next section we briefly summarise what steps they have taken to develop competition laws, and how those laws have been enforced.

4. The plan of the book

Each of the countries with which we are concerned has enacted a major competition law since 1990. In Poland, a law on counteracting monopoly practices was passed in February 1990 and created the Anti-Monopoly Office. In the CSFR a Competition Protection Act was passed in January 1991, establishing an Office for Economic Competition, operating both at

Table 1.3 Legislation governing inward investment in the CSFR, Hungary and Poland

	CSFR 1990, amendments in 1991	HUNGARY 1988, amendments in March 1991	POLAND June, 1991
Date of legislation			
Prerequisites	In most cases only registration of a business is required, in some cases (eg establishing financial institutions, international shipping) government permission is required. It requires waiting up to 6 months while various different offices consider the proposal.	Registration of the business, virtually all activities are opened to foreign business (subject to the decision of the court which registers a company).	Minimum capital required Z110m (less than $1000); Administrative permission required for some specified areas of activity (eg management of airports, real estate brokerage and conveyance, wholesale trade of imported consumer goods). In some areas license is required (eg excavation of minerals, trade of precious metals, production of spirits and tobacco products.
Maximum of foreign ownership	100%	100%	100%
Restrictions on repatriations of profits	None	Profits may be freely transferred in the currency of the original investment.	None

Table 1.3 cont.

	CSFR 1990, amendments in 1991	HUNGARY 1988, amendments in March 1991	POLAND June, 1991
Date of legislation			
Tax benefits	If foreign equity is greater than 30% then tax on profits over Kr200000 is 40% as compared to 55% for domestic private industry. For profits under Kr200000 the tax is equal for both foreign and domestic companies (20%). If foreign equity is less than 30% then tax on profits is the same as for domestic companies (55%).	Entitlement to tax benefits occurs if (a) More than half of the gross takings in the relevant year represents the proceeds of the manufacture of goods or services of a hotel erected by the company, (b) the registered capital exceeds Ft50m, (c) the foreign participation is not less than 30%. Tax relief accounts for 60% during the first 5 years and for 40% during the next 5 years (total tax allowance up to 10 years). If the company pursues one of the Particularly Important Activities (specified in the Law, eg electronics, food production, tourism) the tax break accounts for 100% during first 5 years and 60% during next 5 years.	Temporary (until the end of 1993) system of tax credits. Income tax exemptions are limited to incomes from economic activity as described in permission for its formation. The same refers to exemptions from import duties. Minister of Finance is free to grant tax exemptions if the following conditions are met: (a) is not less than ECU2m, (b) the maximum profits from the exemption cannot exceed the value of capital invested, (c) the company acts in a region with high unemployment, or introduces new technologies, or its exports account for at least 20% of total sales.
Restrictions on property rights	Virtually no restrictions, but there is a casual clause allowing for regulations for reasons of security of state (not defined). However, there may be some restrictions (eg on employment of foreigners governed by other regulations).	Work permit and approval of local authorities is required to employ foreign workers. Non-resident employees may transfer 50% of their remuneration. If foreign share is less than 20% of Ft5m then regulations on ceilings on remuneration apply.	Permission of local authorities is required to employ foreign workers (Law on employment). A foreign entity can acquire the shares of Polish companies exclusively after obtaining permission from the government authorities.

Table 1.4 Comparison of competition legislation in the CSRF, Hungary and Poland

	CSFR	Hungary	Poland
1. Institutional arrangements			
(a) Law	Competition Protection Act (30.1.91)	Act on the Prohibition of Unfair Market Practices (20.11.90)	Law on Counteracting Monopoly Practices (14.2.90)
(b) Competition authority	Office for Economic Competition	Office for Economic Competition	Anti-Monopoly Office
(c) Members appointed by	Organisational structures to be determined by government	President, at request of Prime Minister	President appointed by Prime Minister
(d) Responsible to	Government	Reports to Parliament	Council of Ministers
(e) Role in privatisation	Must ensure competitive environment	Limited role	Examines privatisation proposals for competitive impact
2. Monopolies and mergers			
(a) Definition of dominant position	30% of turnover in relevant markets	30% market share	30% market share (later raised to 40%)
(b) Restriction on mergers	Void unless approved	Permission required for combined market share >30%	Mergers must be notified
3. Anti-competitive practices prohibited			
(a) Price-fixing	Yes	Yes	Yes
(b) Forced contracts	Yes	Yes	Yes
(c) Exclusive dealing	Yes	Yes	Indirectly
(d) RPM	Yes	Yes with limitations	Indirectly
(e) Refusal to supply	Yes	Yes	Yes
(f) Price discrimination	Yes	No	Yes
(g) Tie-in sales	Yes	Imprecise	Yes
(h) Predatory pricing	Not explicitly		Yes
4. Enforcement			
Remedies available	Fines up to 5% of turnover	Price reduction. Fine equals 1.3–2.0 × profit derived	Price reduction and fines. Reduction in managers' salaries

the federal level and in the two republics – the Czech Lands and Slovakia. In Hungary an Act on the prohibition of unfair market practices was passed in 1990. It created an Office of Economic Competition.

The details of these three laws, and the ways in which they have been applied, are discussed below. But it is useful at this stage to give a brief comparison of some of the major aspects of the legislation; this is done in Table 1.4.

This schematic representation is fleshed out in the chapters which follow this introduction. The first part of the book contains four chapters (and a brief commentary) on competition law and policy in the two republics of the CSFR (the Czech Lands and Slovakia), Hungary and Poland. Three of the chapters are written by the heads of the relevant competition authorities. Although future constitutional arrangements for the CSFR are uncertain, it is likely that current competition law will be broadly maintained whatever the outcome.

The second part contains commentaries on the experience of the three countries. Following a brief overview by Schaffer, Stockmann sets out the main issues confronting the governments concerned and de la Laurencie discusses the relationship of the legislation to EC competition law. Then Van Siclen reviews procedures for restructuring at or before privatisation, with a view to developing competition. Estrin and Cave offer some conclusions in a final chapter.

References

Boner R. A. and Krueger R., *The Basics of Antitrust Policy; A Review of Ten Nations and the European Community*, World Bank Technical Paper Number 160, 1991.

Estrin S., *Self Management: Economic Theory and Yugoslav Practice*, Cambridge, Cambridge University Press, 1983.

Fox E., 'Monopolization and Dominace in the United States and the European Community: Efficiency, Opportunity and Fairness', *Notre Dame Law Review*, Vol. 61, pp. 981–1020, 1986.

Hare P. and Hughes G., 'Industrial Policy and Restructuring in Eastern Europe', *Oxford Review of Economic Policy*, Vol. 8, No. 1, pp. 82–104, Spring 1992.

Langenfeld J. and Blitzer M. W., 'Is Competition Policy the Last Thing Central and Eastern Europe Needs?', *American Journal of International Law and Policy*, Vol. 6: pp 347–398, 1991.

Milanovic B., 1989, *Liberalization and Entrepreneurship*, New York, M E Sharpe.

Rosniki, *Statystyszny Przemysl, 1990*, GUS, Warsaw 1991.

1 HUNGARY'S EXPERIENCE OF COMPETITION POLICY

Ferenc Vissi

In keeping with the principles employed in the Western advanced countries, Hungary's competition policy as set out in the 1990 Act on Competition covers questions of restrictive practices, abuse of dominant positions and control of mergers. But the application of the policy shows several distinctive features compared with Western countries. This is due to the fact that competition policy in Hungary cannot be independent of the Hungarian environment of competition, privatisation and management of the crisis resulting from the country's loss of East European markets. These factors must be taken into consideration in assessing the role of competition policy in Hungary in the present phase of transition.

1. Experience in the implementation of the Act on Competition

The new Act on Competition came into force on 1 January 1991. Some of the experience gained by the Competition Office since it started to operate is of great relevance to competition policy.

In 1991 the Competition Council of the Competition Office passed eleven decisions on the basis of the general clause of the Competition Law, which obliges entrepreneurs to respect the freedom and fairness of economic competition and prohibits unfair economic activities, particularly those offending or jeopardising the legitimate interests of rivals and consumers or contrary to the requirements of fair business practice. As was already clear during the drafting of the law, there are and will be cases where the public interest relating to market competition is violated, even though they are not explicitly regulated in the law. In this sense, the general clause is meant to protect the general freedom and fairness of competition. It greatly promotes enforcement of the spirit of the Competition Law.

In connection with the general clause, the Office has so far encountered two different types of cases. The first type included promotional activities banned by the law on Domestic Trading (spirits, tobacco). Those who pursue this illegal activity put their disciplined and law-abiding competitors at a disadvantage, while at the same time gaining unfair advantages in the market. The second type includes those deceptive activities where it was not possible to prove that the customers were deceived in order to boost the marketability of the given product. These cases are not regulated directly by the other clauses of the Competition Law, but the general clause makes it clear to the players in the market that they have special responsibilities, and that wrong market information (even if it is the result of mistakes) is not permitted to cause damage to competitors in the market.

It is the courts' responsibility to decide whether any given behaviour in the market violates the prohibition of unfair trade. Where the courts establish that an activity is unlawful, they transfer the case to the Competition Office which is responsible for imposing a fine. The aim of the fine is to mete out punishment not only for the damage done to the competitors but also for the violation of public interest relating to the fairness of market competition.

The Competition Law enables the Competition Office to bring legal action on behalf of the injured party, although certain conditions are attached: the breach of law in question must be grave, and it must seriously endanger the integrity of competition. For obvious reasons, the legislators wanted to make injured parties assert their own interests. But the fact that the plaintiffs generally fail to bring legal actions is thought-provoking.

By June 1992, ten cases of alleged unfair competition had been filed with the Competition Office covering impairment of business reputation, unfair procurement and utilisation of business secrets, counterfeiting, retaining of goods and interference in competitive bidding. The Office informed the complainants that the cases fell under the courts' jurisdiction but exercised its right to bring legal action only in one of these cases.

The rules of the Act relating to cartels prohibit concerted action by, or agreements between, competitors that seek to limit or exclude economic competition. The Competition Office had by mid-1992 examined 18 cases involving suspected cartels, and unlawful practice was proved in five cases. In two cases the Office stated that the contemplated cartel agreements were not subject to prohibition, and in the remaining eleven cases it found that no unlawful cartels had been established. The eleven cases can be divided into two sub-groups: in some of them the Office found unlawful stipulations in the relevant agreements, but shifts in the market had prevented the partners to the cartel from translating their agreement into practice, while in other cases cartels were suspected of having been established by groups of enterprises operating under joint management or by joint ventures, but the inquiry found no evidence to confirm that suspicion.

Our inquiries into cartels have shown up the important point that the market is not always transparent to agents within it, who may not even recognise the cartels operating in front of their noses. Often they continue to assume they have no course of action open to them – a situation which they got used to over past decades.

Another important lesson learnt by the Office is that enterprises of a given sector, motivated by commercial insecurity or loss of markets in Eastern Europe, want to be privatised on an individual basis. These enterprises appear to have a greater interest in restoring their liquidity than in welding together a combination of firms in the same market. This leads us to draw the probable conclusion that, with the advance of privatisation, various sectors may evolve an oligopolistic structure, which, once established, will give rise to the danger of 'cartelisation'.

The Act on Competition prohibits abuse of a dominant position. Given the centralised enterprise structure of the Hungarian market, we had anticipated that a large number of cases would fall to be investigated by the Competition Office. Indeed, that came to pass, as in 1991 48 such inquiries were held. The Office gained a wealth of interesting experience in this field as well. In a small number of cases the applicants withdrew their applications in the course of proceedings and refused to co-operate with the Office in the taking of evidence. This behaviour suggests both that some applications are unfounded (which can be established in a relatively short time) and that in some cases the injured parties dare not openly initiate proceedings for fear of future reprisals by enterprises with a greater economic power. As can be seen, commercial relations do not change from one day to the next at the pace permitted by a liberalised environment.

In four cases decisions were made finding abuse of dominant position relating to pricing. One of the most delicate problems in competition law is ascertaining whether price changes result from abuse of dominant position. This problem is world-wide, since the alternative competitive price, following from a non-dominant position, is in many cases not observable. The Competition Office does not intend to act as a price authority, and hence it cannot determine a reasonable market price in the course of its proceedings. All it can do is to establish the extent of abuse. This practice of the Office is not accepted easily by participants in relevant markets, and it is particularly the stronger entrepreneurs who fail to realise that they cannot simply dictate the price of a product to buyers.

In a few inquiries we had to evaluate prices set by entrepreneurs in a monopoly position, but to some degree we were unable, or reluctant, to do so. The individual cases are extremely interesting, and some are due to the absence of regulations to govern statutory or natural monopoly positions. One such case involved a dispute between Hungarian Radio and the Broadcasting Company, in which the Competition Office had to consider the price charged by the Broadcasting Company for transmission. In another case we had to establish the price of thermal water supplied to a swimming bath. These examples show both that the professional skills of the Office staff can be improved by acquaintance with international practice and that it is necessary for the government to regulate the sectors which operate as statutory and natural monopolies, because in the absence of such a regulation it is impossible for some provisions of the Act on Competition to be applied with the required degree of certainty.

The Act on Competition lays down clear rules governing the participation of the Competition Office in the privatisation process. Cases relating to this are very few in number for the following reason. Under the Act, enterprises which intend to merge or enter into an equivalent relationship are required to apply to the Office of Competition for permission in cases where their joint share of the market exceeds 30 per cent or their combined annual sales exceed 10 billion forints. Consequently, legal regulation of competition means that the Competition Office is not involved in privatisation except in controlling the growth of concentration in the market. In this sense, therefore, the Competition Office is essentially bypassed by privatisation. This arrangement is contested by many in Hungary, and, indeed, it has arisen from real underlying problems, both political and economic. The question is whether there is a competitive alternative to privatisation in which a more competitive market structure is established by breaking up enterprises before privatisation. Experience shows that such an alternative, if it exists, takes a long time to implement. Where enterprises had been decentralised prior to privatisation, problems concerning the distribution of property, debt-sharing and the introduction of new management took long years to solve. It turned out that installing new management was a comparatively easy task, while the most serious problem was posed by the settlement of matters concerning property and debts. The latter involved court proceedings which in some cases dragged on for years.

According to Paragraph 60 of the Competition Law, ministers are obliged to consult the Competition Office about any draft law that seeks to limit competition. In the first year, the implementation of this paragraph was not free of contradictions. Since numerous laws on the economy are now being drafted, we have to pass judgement on numerous such issues (some 120–30 in 1991). In fact, we have to review certain issues several times, according to the procedures. Since we established contacts with the ministries at the beginning of the year, the majority of these cases were sent over to us by the ministries themselves, although we also had to send special requests for some of them. Meanwhile, our Office also initiated modifications in certain laws.

Experience shows that the Office is anything but a 'sleeping partner' in preparing legislation. The principle of the freedom of competition which our Office represents is still looked upon as a sensitive issue which the state bodies wish to avoid. One problem in this respect is that the ministries quite often cast doubts on the maturity of the market, and place their confidence instead in those economic organisations favoured by the laws they draft. This is why it is difficult to enforce the principle of the freedom of competition in the draft laws, even though the debates over this issue are not yet fully concluded. There is no denying that competition quite often hurts the interests of, and entails serious risk for, the responsible ministry. It also requires the existence of conditions which are rather difficult to achieve.

2. Dilemmas for competition policy posed by privatisation

As in other countries, privatisation in Hungary is the subject of serious political, social and professional debate. The paths chosen by the different countries of Eastern Europe vary considerably, and despite the enormous volume of relevant writings by Western experts, it is an extremely complex task to give clear assessments of the strategic options made. It is a fact that the type of privatisation in the Western countries in the 1970s and the 1980s cannot serve as a general model and that Western experience can be used to best advantage only in similar sectors. (Thus it can be used in the privatisation of enterprises operating in industries which are natural monopolies, particularly as regards ways of developing competition.) The Hungarian Government has articulated its own strategy for privatisation. The following aspects of Hungarian practice deserve mention.

Privatisation is made complicated or difficult by a number of objective factors, such as the relatively low level of domestic savings, which explains the rather slack internal demand for privatisation. Another hindrance is the out-of-date technology and management in large parts of the economy – a situation which cannot be changed immediately. Thirdly, in the course of transformation, it has not yet proved possible to establish a clear and unambiguous pattern of property rights, and the resultant contradictions cannot be eliminated in the process of privatisation. (Compensation undertaken for political motives is a further factor in Hungary, and problems are also encountered in the exercise of property rights by the state and local government.)

A major element in privatisation policy is to set limits to private ownership in certain areas by determining which enterprises are not subject to privatisation but will remain in full or majority government ownership for the short or medium term.

Since the system establishes no restrictions in principle on foreign ownership, privatisation is naturally governed by foreign demand or aspirations of foreigners to procure markets in Hungary. (A different pattern can be observed only in retail trade and services, which are essentially dominated by internal demand.) Thus the government had no choice but to launch privatisation with no concept of a competition policy which took into account the circumstances arising from the loss of Hungary's East European market. One can also perceive a lack of clear ideas about how to deal with the crisis-affected areas in the course of privatisation.

So far actual privatisations have largely occurred in the potentially competitive sector. In view of the fact that Hungarian enterprises show a high degree of concentration in this sector as well (which means that a large part or the whole of internal supply is accounted for by one producer or a few of them), the process of privatisation is fraught with a variety of problems relating to competition policy. The guidelines adopted by Parliament, which the State Property Agency must follow, contain a requirement to consider possibilities of demonopolisation, but there have been no significant developments in this regard because in a significant number of cases demonopolisation is not a viable policy for various objective reasons.

One such reason is that the Hungarian market is on so small a scale that the optimum size of enterprise exceeds the level of demand in Hungary. In other cases, a particular large enterprise may have had several plants, but they are vertically linked, and an attempt was made to privatise either a particular stage of the vertical process or the enterprise as a whole. It was easy to prove that privatisation by foreigners of one element of that vertical structure would be bound to make the remaining part inoperable and to necessitate liquidation of the unprivatised part. So, privatisation in this case was motivated by a desire to conserve national property, as represented by the whole set of activities, rather than by considerations of competition policy. There were also cases in which a single enterprise in a given sector had several factory units, but some of them made such heavy losses or were so debt-ridden that they could not be separated. This type of privatisation has clearly pointed up the contradiction that reorganisation cannot be undertaken without funds and a prospective market. Under the circumstances, the State Property Agency was guided in privatisation by calculating either the smallest possible economic loss or the highest possible receipts that could be expected in a particular sector. Another important lesson of privatisation is that considerations of competition policy cannot serve as a guide except in the context of a prospective market and of existing demand for privatisation.

3. Creating an environment of competition

The East European countries which are now in the process of transformation, including Hungary, have set the goal of building a market economy. Our new constitution proclaims the freedom to set up enterprises, to acquire property and to run businesses. Underlying this declaration is a recognition of the need to remove the impediments which the former regime set to acquisition of property, because a private economy cannot be created otherwise. The constitutional declaration also implies a need for the economy to rely on competition both as a general value and as a means of promoting welfare, increasing the efficiency of resource allocation and introducing pressures for profitable production.

The Hungarian Government intends to meet these requirements by proclaiming and implementing a property reform, opening the country to foreign competition and removing the obstacles in the way of competition.

The overall collapse of East European markets has caused the Hungarian economy to lose a vast market in a short time, on a scale unparalleled in history. The loss of markets is virtually impossible to make up for, and, because most of the former markets cannot be recovered, it should not be treated as a simple recession. Moreover, the prospects for easing the existing problems are extremely uncertain, and this poses a dilemma both for enterprises and for the economy as a whole. There are various estimates by experts of the extent to which the Hungarian economy can be expected to decline in consequence of the collapse of the East European market. The figures indicate an overall decline of 20 to 40 per cent, with substantial variations among sectors.

Several sectors or enterprises have practically ceased to exist or are in the process of complete liquidation. This situation is of particular relevance to competition policy, because a competition policy as traditionally understood has never been formulated under conditions of collapse of so vast a market. In practice, there is virtually no use in talking of restricting competition in such areas. The experience of the Competition Office shows that these changes have operated to weaken the market power of firms, formerly of great size and dominant in the market, to the extent that they are no longer capable of abusing their dominant position. A high proportion of the metallurgical industry and some firms in the chemical and food industries have 50 to 70 per cent of their capacity unutilised and each of them is preoccupied with exploring avenues for survival. Abuse of a dominant position which would normally be combated by traditional anti-trust policy cannot be part of those enterprises' strategies.

After it took office two years ago, the present government continued the policy of liberalisation which had been embarked upon by its predecessor. This policy had made significant headway in two areas in particular, those of prices and foreign trade.

Price liberalisation in practice took place under the previous government. The ratio of centrally fixed prices fell to 10 per cent of the market as a whole, and the new government inherited a price system and a price structure in which most prices were competitive ones. This was the most important (but not the sole) reason that shock therapy was not applied. In fact inflation gathered speed in 1990 and 1991, but the underlying cause is not to be found in the price liberalisation policy pursued in those years. In November 1990 the present government submitted to Parliament a draft law on price control. Passed by Parliament, this law clearly defines a narrow scope for government intervention in prices and specifies the groups of products subject to official prices, which currently represent some 8 per cent of total consumption. In addition, the Price Law states that the right to set prices lies with business. It has repealed all existing laws and regulations on prices, thereby achieving a significant degree of deregulation.

On the basis of that law one can say that the government retains its price-fixing powers essentially in respect of the so-called natural monopolies and in some specific areas like a few major agricultural products.

Liberalisation in the field of foreign trade started in 1989. The previous government first liberalised technology imports and then secondly imports of primary and semi-finished products. Under the present government, liberalisation has increasingly been extended to the import of consumer goods. Foreign trade licences are now required only for a very small group of products, mainly those governed by international agreements or in areas where foreign trade is subject to special restrictions or procedural rules (e.g. the arms trade). During the past two years, import liberalisation has resulted in essential shifts in the Hungarian market. The shortage economy has practically vanished. Import competition has displaced domestic production in several areas or has led to a market decline in prices in some fields. Apart from minimum restrictions, foreign trade has become a basic economic right.

The freedom of foreigners to establish firms can be viewed in the context of liberalisation. Repatriation of profit is subject to no restriction and founding companies or firms carries with it various benefits.

These measures of liberalisation have been instrumental in establishing an environment of competition. Their benefits overall are accompanied by some adverse consequences which the government could not make timely preparations to meet and which may cause some loss to society and the economy. Since the government had no well-developed plan to save certain sectors from drastic declines by following the international practice of protectionism, liberalisation has had the effect of causing steep declines in or even the extinction of certain sectors. It is still a subject to debate in Hungary whether a more gradual process of liberalisation could have prevented a decline in domestic capacity and the very rapid growth of unemployment. It seems to me that this debate cannot be decided now, and that only after a lapse of a few years will it be possible to form a more accurate evaluation of the positive and negative effects.

2 COMPETITION POLICY IN THE POLISH ECONOMY IN TRANSITION

Anna Fornalczyk

1. Introduction to the Polish situation

Monopolisation and highly concentrated markets are a troublesome heritage from central planning. Large, multi-plant firms were set up to implement plans which were established at the national level. During this period, state monopolies flourished behind a wall of protective measures and subsidies.

The transformation process from a centrally planned economy to a fully fledged market economy started in 1990 in Poland. The main goals have been stabilisation of the economy and structural changes in both production and the organisation of the economy as a whole. Stabilisation was a prerequisite to eradicate the phenomenon of shortage as soon as possible and took the form of monetary stabilisation without substantive structural changes, at least at the outset.

The stabilisation programme has created a new economic environment for firms. The main feature of this change has been a significant decrease of demand, which has eliminated shortage. In principle our enterprises should adapt their behaviour in this new environment, but the majority of firms have not done so. This is because they have acquired the habit of producing without respect for the requirements of purchasers or consumers. Moreover, they survived numerous reforms in the past and think they can survive these: they are waiting for the collapse of the current reform. In other words, they have implemented a so-called 'tactic of survival'.

However, some firms have begun to adapt to the new circumstances, and they have had some good results. These results were often closely connected with changes of organisational structure and with the privatisation process. Some companies have also gained a handsome profit, primarily because of their dominant position in the domestic market. Ownership and organisational change will not of itself necessarily decrease market monopolisation. Firms would certainly not like to weaken their own market position. This suggests that demonopolisation should be one of the most important goals of government policy.

The high level of monopoly power has been a structural source of inflation. When demand did increase, in the second half of 1990, the monopolies' first response was to increase prices. It has been also the reason for the lack, as yet, of a positive side to recession in the Polish economy. In market economies, recession is argued to cleanse the economy of inefficient firms. As demand falls, so does production. This results in an increase of average costs, due to the rise of fixed costs' share in a global cost of production. In a market economy the least efficient producers are pushed out of the market. The situation is different in a monopolised economy, where producers are more easily able to shift the costs of recession to customers. This explains the emergence of high inflation in the Polish economy and the relatively good economic performance of monopolies, in the sense of an ability to survive recession rather than high profitability.

The lack of competition and the necessity for organisational changes in the economy stimulated the Polish Parliament to pass the Anti-Monopoly Law in February 1990. On 13 April 1990 the Anti-Monopoly Office was established as a government agency, which is in charge of enforcement of the Anti-Monopoly Law. The Office is responsible for counteracting restrictive business practices and for structural changes in the economy as a whole. The Office is headed by a President appointed and dismissed by the Prime Minister. The activity of the Office covers two substantive spheres: jurisdiction and anti-monopoly policy. The Department of Judgments deals with counteracting restrictive business practices. The Department of Anti-Monopoly Policy deals with premerger notifications, approvals of firms' privatisation, splitting up firms and analysis of market monopolisation.

Generally speaking, the Anti-Monopoly Law has been introduced in order:

i.   to protect economic entities against monopolistic practices;
ii. to secure the interests of consumers;
iii. to help all producers and trade enterprises to compete freely with each other on the basis of quality and prices.

There are two substantive provisions of the Anti-Monopoly Law. Chapter 2 prohibits anti-competitive practices and Chapter 3 deals with structural change. Chapter 2 defines restrictive business practices which can result from an abuse of a dominant position of companies in the market or from restrictive agreements between competitors to set prices or output or to cartelise the market. Chapter 3 of the Law covers mergers and acquisitions, ownership changes and creation of new firms. Such undertakings are prohibited where they would result in market dominance. Apart from that, dominant enterprises can be broken up on the decision of the Offices. This would be possible where the activity of the firm reduces real or potential competition.

The Anti-Monopoly Office in Poland does not have a long tradition. In spite of this, its experience is already relatively rich. It has made over 150 decisions related to restrictive business practices and received over 1,000 applications concerning the privatisation process, restructuring of firms and mergers. None the less, the results of these activities are a drop in an ocean, in the context of the high level of monopolisation of the Polish market.

The establishment of the Anti-Monopoly Office aroused high expectations, associated with a hope for rapid demonopolisation of the economy. However, various factors have constrained its possibilities in practice. Some of these have been connected with a lack of knowledge of competition policy; others have been a result of specific features of the transformation process.

In the following section I summarise the Polish Anti-Monopoly Law, and recent legislative developments. The activities of the Anti-Monopoly Office are discussed in the third section, while in the fourth I try to reflect on differences between competition policy in a fully fledged market economy and one in an economy in transformation from a centrally planned system to a market one. Conclusions are drawn in the final section.

2. The Polish Anti-Monopoly Law

The Polish Anti-Monopoly Law was passed in 1990. The goals outlined in its preamble are 'to ensure the development of competition, to protect economic entities from monopolistic practices and to protect the interests of consumers'. The law forbids certain monopolistic practices, unless they are 'necessary to conduct an economic activity and do not result in a significant restraint of competition'. They include:

1. agreements to fix prices, share markets, limit production, or deny market access to other firms;
2. abuse of a dominant position (this would be the position of a firm that 'does not encounter significant competition'; it is presumed to pertain if firms have a 40 per cent market share), such as preventing the emergence of competition, division of the market on territorial or product criteria, refusals to sell or purchase when there are no alternatives, and certain forms of price discrimination; and
3. single firm conduct, such as imposing onerous contract terms that yield undue benefit, acquiring securities or assets of other firms if it results in a significant weakening of competition and establishing an interlocking directorate with a competitor.

The law additionally prohibits firms with a monopolistic position (i.e. one that 'does not encounter significant competition') from:

i. limiting production, sale, or purchase, despite having adequate capacity;

ii. refraining from sale of commodities to increase prices; and
iii. charging excessively exorbitant prices.

A firm that is found to have committed a monopolistic practice may be ordered to cease and fined up to 15 per cent of its revenue for the previous year.

Mergers and transformations (commercialisations and privatisations) must be notified to the Office. Within two months of notification, the Office may forbid the action if it would create or maintain a dominant position. Firms with a dominant position may be divided if they 'permanently restrain competition'. Cases are initiated either by complaint or by the Office on its own initiative.

The Anti-Monopoly Office is a part of the government, subordinated to the Council of Ministers. The Office is headed by a President and a Vice President appointed by the Prime Minister. The President attends meetings of the Council of Ministers. The Office employs altogether 110 persons, 74 of whom work in the Warsaw headquarters, and has three main departments. The Department of Anti-Monopoly Judgments is responsible for investigating and preparing decisions on monopolistic practices. The Department of Anti-Monopoly Policy, Analysis and Supervision is responsible for reviewing and preparing decisions on structural matters. The Legal Department renders legal advice and defends Office decisions in the Anti-Monopoly Court. There are 7 regional offices, located in Gdansk, Katowice, Krakow, Lublin, Lodz, Poznan, and Wroclaw. From January 1992, regional offices are responsible for making decisions on cases originating in their regions, unless the case involves national or inter-regional markets or certain specialised issues that are always handled in Warsaw.

In practice, the main activities of the Anti-Monopoly Office are:

1. supervising the observance of the law and regulations countering monopolistic practices by firms;
2. reviewing the formation of prices under conditions of restrained competition;
3. issuing, in cases pursuant to this Act, decisions on counteracting monopolistic practices and shaping the organisational structure of economic entities and decisions specifying the liability of entities for engaging in such practices;
4. registering economic entities whose share of the national market exceed 80 per cent;
5. conducting research on the state of concentration of the economy and presenting to the relevant entities conclusions on suggested actions to attain a market equilibrium;
6. drafting or advising on draft proposals for new laws concerning monopolistic practices or the development of competition or the conditions for its emergence;
7. preparing government proposals for a policy for developing competition.

The 1990 Anti-Monopoly Law was amended in June 1991 as follows:

1. the market share that presumptively establishes that a firm has a dominant position was changed from 30 per cent to 40 per cent;
2. the Anti-Monopoly Office was permitted to block a structural change that would 'maintain' a dominant position, as well as those that would create a dominant position;
3. the burden of proof was clarified in certain 'rule of reason' cases: when a party claims that a practice is justified because it is necessary to conduct an economic activity and does not result in a significant restraint of competition, the burden of proving that such circumstances exist is on the party who claims that they exist;
4. individuals may be fined up to six months' salary if they refuse to provide information in response to an Office demand, or provide false information, or if they do not make the required notification of a structural change;
5. the Office is permitted to reject any complaint that on its face does not have merit, rather than being required to prepare a formal decision;
6. decisions on monopolistic practices may not be issued more than 12 months after the end of the year in which the practice ceased.

3. The enforcement of competition law and policy: a summary of activities

During 1991, 83 legal proceedings were started by the Anti-Monopoly Office, 113 decisions were pronounced (including decisions on cases which commenced the preceding year), and 5 cases were concluded with mutual conciliations between the concerned parties (that were accepted by the Office). Apart from these, 258 interventions were undertaken in cases not requiring formal administrative procedures.

73 out of the 83 administrative proceedings were initiated at the request of a subject entitled to demand an institution of such proceedings, and 10 were initiated by the Anti-Monopoly Office itself. Within the group of 73 proceedings initiated on the request, in 69 cases requests were made by economic entities. In 70 of the 113 decisions, there was a finding that there were no monopolistic practices, and in 23 cases the matter was discontinued because additional investigation disclosed no basis for any formal proceeding. As for the remaining 20 decisions, all of the alleged monopolistic practices were found in 14 cases and some were found in 6 cases.

Most of the decisions of the Office concerned counteracting anti-competitive practices defined in Art. 4.1.1 of the Act as imposing onerous terms of contracts that yield undue benefits to the economic entity imposing them (50 decisions). Another 18 decisions concerned Art. 4.1.2., which prohibits making the conclusion of a contract contingent on forcing the other party to accept or perform another service not connected with the object of the contract, which would not otherwise be accepted or performed if there were a choice. In an additional 16 cases, the decision finding or not finding a violation was based on both of these articles.

Over 70 per cent of the Office's decisions dealt with unilateral practices by economic entities that usually did not have dominant or monopolistic positions. Monopolistic practices by dominant or monopolistic entities (covered by Art. 5 and 7) were the subject of 20 per cent of the decisions, and monopolistic agreements (covered by Art. 4.2) – mainly vertical ones – were the subject of 10 per cent of the decisions. No decisions were issued on the basis of Art 4.1.3 (controlling acquisition of stocks or assets of economic entities), or Art. 4.1.4 (prohibiting persons from holding certain positions in competing economic entities). Additionally, in accordance with Art. 15 and 16, two fines were imposed. One was imposed on an economic entity for violating an order to cease monopolistic practices; the other fine was imposed on a managing person for failing to provide information.

Proceedings initiated against enterprises taking advantage of their position as natural monopolists (producers and suppliers of electricity, central heating, natural gas and telecommunications) turned out to be very numerous and time-consuming for the Anti-Monopoly Office. Therefore, it was decided to establish within the Jurisdiction Department a special team to deal with such cases. The team pronounced 32 decisions. In 16 cases the Office found that there were no monopolistic practices, and in 8 cases proceedings were discontinued because the investigation found no evidence sustaining the initial complaints. Of the remaining 8 cases, there were 4 decisions finding that all of the alleged monopolistic practices had occurred, 3 decisions finding that some monopolistic practices had occurred, but not all that had been alleged, and 1 in which a decision imposed a fine for failure to provide information. In addition to these cases involving abuse of natural monopoly position, the Office recommended to other government agencies the adoption of a different and better system for regulating natural monopolies. The Office concentrated on the energy sector, and it proposed changes in some regulations and made more general long-term proposals.

Many times in the course of proceedings the Office had to interpret provisions of the Act, drawing also from the interpretations of the Anti-Monopoly Court. In particular, interpretations were necessary concerning the:

i. scope of application of the Act; one of the important problems was to determine what entities are covered by it – for example, whether the Act applied to local self-government institutions or municipal enterprises performing economic functions;
ii. substantive provisions of the Act; defining such terms as 'excessively exorbitant price', 'unfair influence on price formation', and 'significant competition' turned out to be quite difficult.

The calibre of the Office's decisions can be evaluated from the way the Anti-Monopoly Court rules on appeals from those decisions. Among a total of 17 appeals against decisions pronounced by the Jurisdiction Department of the Office (3 in 1990 and 14 in 1991), the Court issued 13 decisions:

- 7 decisions of the Office were upheld, and 1 proceeding was discontinued because an appeal was withdrawn;
- 4 decisions of the Office were reversed;
- 1 decision was changed in part.

As of the end of 1991, there were 4 appeals pending in the Anti-Monopoly Court.

To give a feel for the problems being handled by the Office, it may be useful to indicate some of the more significant cases:

i.   *Case No. Do I-500-24/91* was initiated by the Office against two enterprises, Factory of Enamel Pots and Production-Trade Enterprise 'Uplex'. Both enterprises entered agreements which provided 'Uplex' with exclusive sales rights for the factory's products in a local geographic market. This factory has a dominant position in the overall Polish market. This exclusive contract did not aim at improving quality. The Office ordered that this practice cease, because it was a monopolistic agreement restraining access to the market.

ii. *Case No. Do I-500-6/91* was initiated on request of Housing Cooperative 'Przyszlosc' ('Future') in Opole against Voivodship (provincial government) Enterprise of Water Pipes and Sewage in Opole. The Enterprise was a natural monopolist and was imposing unequal terms of contract on its customers. Among other things, it was not taking responsibility for the worsening of water quality. The Office, and then the Anti-Monopoly Court on appeal, both concluded that imposing such unequal terms is an individual monopolistic practice.

iii. *Case No. Do I-500-59/90* was initiated on the request of Craftsman Chamber in Poznan against the branch of PZU (Polish National Insurance) operating in Pila. It was found that PZU had agreements with chosen firms that provide repair services and PZU was directing its customers to them, which led to the elimination of other firms on the market. The Office ordered that this practice cease.

iv. *Case No. Do I-644-72/90* was initiated by the Office against Zagan Wool Processing Enterprise in Zagan. At first it appeared that prices had been increased significantly and production reduced. During further proceedings, monopolistic practices were not found. Output had been reduced because of a drastic demand decrease.

The Anti-Monopoly Office has also been concerned with influencing market structures and with monitoring privatisation, restructuring and new firms. Since its formation, the Office has received 1,089 applications concerning the transformation or creation of economic entities. The pattern of applications is summarised in Table 2.1.

Table 2.1 The pattern of applications for enterprise transformation

Concerns	No. of Cases	Percentage of Cases
Manufacturing Industry	552	51
Agriculture	198	18
Trade and Services	129	12
Construction	100	9
Publishing	36	3
Municipal Enterprises	28	3
Design Offices	18	2
Banks	9	1
Telecommunications	9	1
Other	10	1
Total	1089	101

To simplify the procedure of 'commercialisation' (formally the transformation of enterprises into one-person joint stock companies of the state treasury), the Office, together with the Ministry of Ownership Changes, worked out a set of standard procedures. In doubtful cases, the Office first negotiated a settlement with the involved party and then made a formal decision. The goal was to modify the transformation process in a manner favourable for competition. This procedure in practice led to issuing so-called conditional 'decisions', which imposed on the Office an obligation to monitor the transformation processes. There were 60 opinions of this conditional type, 52 of them addressed to entities not connected with agriculture. In 1991, 15 industrial enterprises were monitored, of which there were some reservations about the implementation of the conditions in three.

Within the mass commercialisation process, the Office examined 89 individual applications. In addition, the Ministry of Ownership Changes presented a much longer list of enterprises that were candidates for a mass commercialisation, and the Office objected in 100 cases, mainly monopolists, and enterprises operating in agriculture and energy.

The Office also worked on ways to direct the important process of transformation through liquidation. Liquidation is a form of privatisation in which a company is formally dissolved, but all or part of its assets are transferred to a new private company that carries on its business. In such cases, the Office demands information from the founding institutions of liquidated entities to determine whether, as a result of this acquisition, the buyer will gain a dominant position. However, the Anti-

Monopoly Law does not currently wield sufficient authority to control such liquidations directly. It is expected that this problem will be addressed in the forthcoming amendments to the law. The Offices also gave support to subordinate units of large enterprises that wished to be separated from their parent firms, especially entities having a dominant or monopolistic position within the meaning of the Act. Such actions were undertaken in five cases.

The role of the Office in the transformation process is well illustrated by the case of a wood enterprise from the north-east of Poland. This firm notified the Office of its intention to transform into a one-person joint stock company of the state treasury. Based on submitted documents, the Anti-Monopoly Office found out that it was a multi-plant enterprise, consisting of twenty sawmills organised into twelve production divisions (each with partially separate accounts and some independence), where 7 of the divisions had more than one sawmill in different locations; a service unit; and two units dealing with sales. During further proceedings it turned out that the market share of this producer on the local market for hardwood lumber production was 98.1 per cent, and for softwood lumber production, 99.8 per cent. In the opinion of the Office, the production capacity of the enterprise and its well-established market position created barriers to entry in the market. The Office therefore prohibited transformation of this enterprise. The enterprise appealed against the decision to the Anti-Monopoly Court, which considered the following questions:

- did the Office act according to the appropriate article of the Anti-Monopoly Act?
- what was the relevant geographic market of the enterprise – nation-wide or local?
- was a dominant position of the enterprise in production and sales of lumber proved?

The Court did not find any failure in the action taken by the Office with reference to conduct of this proceeding, agreed with arguments presented by the Office and rejected the appeal of the enterprise. Thus, the enterprise was obliged to prepare a new plan complying with the Anti-Monopoly Law. The Office does not however, have the power to prescribe a particular form of division in transformation cases.

The Office has also been involved in attempting to influence emerging market structures by dividing up dominant firms. Decisions on divisions in 1991 dealt mainly with the grain-mill industry. A group of seventeen enterprises was identified in 1990 and the division process started in 1991. Eleven decisions were issued, specifying rules for dividing assets and deadlines. As a result, between three and thirteen independent entities emerged from each of the original enterprises. Five enterprises appealed against the rulings, and in one case an appeal was made by a voivoda (provincial official nominated by the Prime Minister). So far the Anti-Monopoly Court has examined four cases and upheld the Office's decision in each one. For the remainder of the seventeen enterprises the proposal to divide an enterprise was once abandoned and in two cases, conditional consent was given on the basis of restructuring concepts presented by the enterprise. In two cases, the procedure is suspended until property rights are clarified.

A typical example of the dividing activities of the Office is a case of PZZ (Polish Cereal Enterprises) Ciechanow. This enterprise was on the list of seventeen enterprises to be broken up. After consultation with representatives of the enterprise, the Anti-Monopoly Office issued a decision ordering division of the enterprise. It suggested creating 4 new entities but under the law this proposal is not obligatory and PZZ Ciechanow appealed against the decision to the Anti-Monopoly Court. In practice the Court supported our suggestion but changed the deadline, postponing it for six months.

However, despite expectations to the contrary, the Office did not put into effect a broad, radical deconcentration policy. The caution of the Office was a result of the belief that division procedures are very slow by their nature and that there is a major threat of making a mistake, since it is hard to define a proper balance between a more competitive structure and possible loss of advantages of economies of scale and scope. To diminish the probability of errors, the Anti-Monopoly Office undertook a general study of the affected industry prior to commencement of the division process. For example, next year a special sectoral study is planned for seed production, prior to a proposed division process. The Office experience suggests that there is a threat of reconcentration if the division process is not an element of a deeper restructuring and privatisation process for the whole industry. This, for example, occurred in the sugar industry.

4. Reflections on competition policy in market and transition economies

When we think about the conduct of competition policy in the Polish economy in transition, in comparison with a market economy, we can isolate the following key differences. First, some provisions of the Anti-Monopoly Law make our activity more difficult than it would be in a market economy without a centrally planned past. Second, competition means more troubles for enterprises. Frequently they are facing bankruptcy and they try to survive by any means. The weak condition of Polish firms does not allow us to take strict anti-trust measures. Third, there are many short term conflicts between competition policy and restructuring programmes, even though ultimately competition policy is vital to a true restructuring of the Polish economy.

The wide scope of responsibilities provided in the Anti-Monopoly Law was motivated by the high concentration ratios in Polish product markets. At first, the Office was obliged to start an investigation on each case received. This obligation was a direct consequence of the 'economy of shortage', because the lack of goods on the market gave a dominant position to almost every company. Then, 'the economy of shortage' disappeared more quickly than the authors of the Anti-Monopoly Law had foreseen. In consequence claims of restrictive business practices, which often related to firms which no longer had a dominant position on a local or national market, still had to be investigated. Last year the Anti-Monopoly Court annulled one decision, because it did not have significant bearing on demonopolisation. Because of this experience, the Office initiated an amendment to the Law passed by Parliament in June 1991. This allows for the rejection of complaints that do not have merit, without undertaking a formal investigation. Since September 1991, claims have been selected in a way calculated to make the Office's activity more effective.

As we have seen, the Anti-Monopoly Law also provides for strong legal control of structural changes in the economy. It embraces a notification procedure for the privatisation of state-owned firms; for mergers; and for setting up new firms that may reach a dominant position on a market. Every such case must be notified to the Anti-Monopoly Office. The overwhelming number of these applications were accepted without question because the firms had a low market share. But this preventive activity has been time-consuming and has not left enough time for as much *ex officio* activity as is required. The Office believes that there are too many large firms with dominant positions on markets and some of them should be divided as soon as possible.

Division of firms is a complex and controversial method of competition policy. Sometimes the Office's decisions have been criticised. Opponents often claim that large and powerful companies exist in market economies in Western countries, so Office decisions have been seen as a factor weakening Polish enterprises' position on the international market.

We do not doubt that this criticism is based on a misunderstanding. First, we are aware that large companies play a very important role in market economies, but the substantive difference between post-communist and market monopolies is the way in which they reached this position. If a company reached this position by a struggle on the market against other competitors, its behaviour on the market has been quite different from a company that received a dominant position by a decision of the state administration. The dominant positions enjoyed by the overwhelming majority of our firms were given to them by the state administration. Thus, they do not know a lot about market behaviour. The best example has been enterprises' failure to react to the lack of demand in the two-year transitional period following the stabilisation programme in Poland. We used to say that the monopolies in a fully-fledged market economy have not been strong because of their size, but they have become large and powerful because of their market skills. We are deeply convinced that even though the division of large multi-plant state-owned firms very often would bring some early problems, in the long run they would benefit from the knowledge of modern management and a market-oriented strategy. They would also be better prepared for competition on the international market. This is a case in which there is a discrepancy between long-term and short-term interests. Government economic policies should concentrate on the former. The Anti-Monopoly Office has insisted on an expansion of market forces in the economy and other ministries have often treated us like a trouble-maker. Of course, we are none the less open to rational arguments concerning the restructuring process of our economy.

There are also potential conflicts between the goals of the restructuring process and competition policy in the short run. Over two years, the Polish government has commenced numerous restructuring programmes in various fields of the economy. The studies have focused on the technical and economic aspects of firms' activities. Unfortunately they have also been prepared to support the realisation of firms' goals, which rarely take competition into account. Indeed, a competitive market would usually cause additional problems in the implementation of the recommendations. The authors of these programmes have tried to avoid discussion of competition problems. Nobody likes competition in his own backyard. Despite this experience, it would not make much sense now to prepare parallel sectoral studies focused on competition problems because of the cost, in time and money. Representatives of the Anti-Monopoly Office have, however, contributed to discussions on the substantive goals of the restructuring programmes, and tried to inject some competition rules into them. Our participation in the final part of the work has often delayed the studies' preparation process. Time would have been saved if we had been involved from the outset.

We are aware that there are conflicts between competition and industrial policy in market economies as well. The difference is one of degree in an economy in transition. We must transform the bulk of our economy in a relatively short time; we are in a hurry, but should avoid big mistakes. One of the biggest would be restructuring the economy without competition. A second important constraint on our efforts is resistance to import liberalisation. Many of our companies have faced bankruptcy for more than a year. Imports have been threatening for them because of their weak economic state and their slow adaptation to the new market. Firms' economic problems derive from a lack of demand following stabilisation. In general, most branches lost a significant share of their market, because of hard budget constraints for purchasers and households that, in turn, resulted in decreased demand. An additional reason for the decline of sales was the breakup of trade relations with the former Soviet Union and the breakup of the CMEA. We have had economic shock therapy for more than two years.

Following the logic of this therapy, the Anti-Monopoly Office initiated in 1990 a decrease of import tariffs for goods in highly monopolised markets. It improved competition but at the same time brought a higher deficit in the balance of payments. It also caused a lot of financial problems for firms. New customs duties were introduced in August 1991 and the average import duty has gone up from about 8 per cent to 17 per cent. Western countries have experienced similar problems, especially during recession. But the problem has been more serious in Poland, because it has been more wide-reaching. On a related issue, one can stress the important role of the Association Agreement between the EEC and Poland, which set up a gradual implementation of free trade rules. This ensures our enterprises will have time to adapt to changing conditions. The process will also need big efforts from the bottom and from the top. By the bottom I refer to the implementation of restructuring programmes at a micro-economic level. The programmes should aim to improve technology and management, to decrease costs of production and to apply more attention to quality and innovation. The top in this context means that government policies should influence the restructuring of the economy as whole. The policies should create proper conditions for enterprises' activity and should not permit firms to survive without these changes.

The next issue concerns foreign investors' requirements when they start to do business in Poland. Foreign investors and our own companies demand protection of the Polish domestic market. This is one of the most common requests, and represents a serious dilemma for us. We need foreign capital, know-how and new methods of management, but cannot allow monopolisation of the Polish market by foreign firms. So far, we have accepted some temporary solutions for particular investment projects and when we discuss a level of protection, typically it is not high.

Our other important occupation is privatisation. The Anti-Monopoly Office is responsible for demonopolisation through organisational changes following the transformation of state-owned companies into private ones. As mentioned above, firms are obliged to submit applications to the Office when they are to be privatised. We co-operate with the Ministry for Ownership Changes and help to select enterprises for mass privatisation. For example, last year over one hundred enterprises were removed from an official list prepared by the Ministry. Some were removed because of our projects related to the sectoral studies in the agriculture industry and the wood manufacturing industry. Firms in the energy sector were removed from the outset because we have been convinced that this sector needs general solutions, given its key role in the economy as a whole. The main problem is methods of regulation and this could be resolved by implementing the results of a sectoral study carried out by foreign experts. The electricity supply industry and the gas industry are regulated in market economies as well. For the petrol industry, which has been monopolised in Poland for many years, we insisted on a change in organisational structure. The sectoral study of the industry is complete and for a few months we have discussed which is the best of two options. The first protects the industry from competition, especially foreign competition, and the government must set up new non-tariff barriers. This special control over petrol imports was justified via the provision of excise duty; the government wanted to stop illegal imports and earn revenues for the budget. The Anti-Monopoly Office accepts the fiscal argument but instead promotes the second option: reorganisation of the industry. This option involves setting up two independent companies for petrol production and distribution. Each of them should compete with the other. It does not mean closing the market to import competition, but the economy will be opened only gradually; as the companies grow stronger, import barriers should be lifted. In September of 1992 the Council of Ministers made the decision to carry out the second option.

Recession, unemployment and the weak condition of Polish firms has led to the formation of crisis cartels. This new form of companies' co-operation means that they back each other and avoid expensive bank credits as far as it is possible. It means also that they avoid judicial procedures to extract payments following delivery of products. This has been a serious problem in our economy for more than a year. Purchasers have been unwilling to pay for goods they have received. Above all, they spent the money on salaries. This has been increasingly common since the beginning of the economic reform, and has caused an insolvency of suppliers which has spread throughout the economy. The crisis cartels support this strategy.

We have obtained information on firms' joint undertakings, focused on horizontal agreements on price or other trade conditions. The best example, and the newest one, is the sugar manufacturing industry. Three years ago, i.e., before the Anti-Monopoly Office was established, a country-wide organisation in this industry was abolished by decision of the Ministry of Finance, and since then independent sugar manufacturing companies have operated in the market. The idea behind this division was to let the market select which firms were efficient and which were inefficient. It did not happen, because of a crisis cartel focused on a joint price policy. We have known about it for several months, but an investigation and the evidence needed by the Anti-Monopoly Court takes time to amass. We have chosen another way, by preventing legalisation of this cartel. First of all, we requested an elimination of inefficient firms, because of their influence on average costs of production in the sugar manufacturing industry as a whole. Instead, we have faced requests for higher tariff barriers and export subsidies without any substantive changes in the industry. The sectoral study proposed that several joint stock companies should be set up in this industry and should compete on the basis of their costs of production, but a strong lobby seeks a reconstruction of the old organisational structure without competition. This group often uses the example of Western countries, which have long regulated and subsidised this industry. The Anti-Monopoly Office argues that we have different goals at this stage of market oriented reform.

A price cartel is one kind of restrictive business practice. Others include excessive prices, exclusive distributorship agreements, setting up barriers to new entry, tied selling and strong conditions on payment imposed by dominant firms on weaker purchasers and consumers. The Anti-Monopoly Office is charged to counter these practices. But as in our other activities, decisions against these practices often put firms in a very difficult economic situation. Sometimes, enterprises would not be able to exist without these practices. The best example is a car factory case undertaken when we began our operations. The company increased car prices three times within one month following an increase in costs of production and a rapid rise in demand. It was the exclusive producer of middle-size cars, with a dominant position on the domestic market, protected by customs duties. Our decision ordered a decrease of prices, but the Anti-Monopoly Court did not share our arguments. Its judgement stated that we had not proved that the prices had been excessive. The Anti-Monopoly Court decided that the firm could set prices according to costs of production, the level of demand and profit adequate to the firm's needs. Of course, this would be understandable in a competitive market, but in the Office's view, in the Polish situation it means freedom for monopolies and creates cost-push inflation. Monopolistic prices also reflect producers' inefficiency. We appealed, but the Supreme Court supported the judgement, though its argument focused on different aspects of the case. First, the Supreme Court considered that the company could increase prices because an import tariff barrier protected the domestic car producer. The Anti-Monopoly Office as a government agency should follow government policies as a whole. Second, an increase of prices was not a monopolistic practice, but a consequence of unskilled management. We have begun to use these arguments to explain our reluctant approach to price control and our efforts to relax various import constraints. When we started the investigation, we supposed that the administrative way would take longer and not be so effective as the market way. Before making the decision, we initiated a formal procedure concerning a relaxation of import barriers for cars. This was in fact done by the government, and imports increased rapidly, bringing a stronger demand barrier on the domestic market. It influenced the companies' behaviour and car prices were stabilised. New higher customs duties were introduced last year and were increased this year again. These increases were connected with the requests of foreign investors which intended to set up joint ventures with Polish companies.

We therefore come back to the problems of restructuring the economy and the inflow of foreign capital. There is visible feedback between competition policy and different aspects of the transition process. As long as the majority of our dominant firms are facing bankruptcy, counteracting restrictive business practices cannot be effective. This does not mean we should be tolerant, but rather that we should focus our activity on the causes of these practices. In other words, we should initiate and support undertakings to make organisational changes in our economy which are an important element in its demonopolisation, and insist on relaxation of import tariffs and non-tariff barriers.

5. Conclusions

Monopolisation in post-communist countries has been an important obstacle in the transformation to a market system. Awareness of this fact leads to a number of undertakings for the elimination of monopolistic structures. The structural approach to the competition policy has prevailed, and is seen as a substantive approach to the economic policy of the government.

Demonopolisation and privatisation of the economy should not be treated as goals, but as ways to improve economic efficiency. Therefore, companies ought to be encouraged in their attempts to diminish costs of production, improve quality of products and implement innovations. The breaking up of firms is justified when it leads to the creation of a competitive market. Privatisation should lead to the emergence of a well-defined owner, ready to take economic risks and accept the positive and negative consequences of this activity. Excessive dispersion of ownership rights will not assure the emergence of efficient owner control over the managers in a privatised firm, particularly given the lack of a developed capital market.

Monopolisation of the economy and likely changes in the economic system imply that competition policy in Poland in the coming years will consist of: demonopolisation of the economy (connected where possible with privatisation of firms); the creation of conditions for the economy to be open to foreign competition (foreign investors and competitive imports); and organisational and financial support for the development of small business. The opening of the economy to foreign co-operation is very important, because of the relatively small scale of the domestic market in Poland, which makes the deconcentration of domestic production unprofitable in many fields.

To summarise, the Polish Anti-Monopoly Office faces many problems. Some of them are the same as are faced by competition agencies in market economies, for example established enterprises wishing to be exempted from competitive forces. Many are quite different, such as influencing the restructuring of state monopolies and dealing with an economic decline that has both macro-economic and micro-economic origins. We hope to use the same analytical tools as our market economy colleagues, but must remember that the situation is quite different.

3 COMPETITION AND COMPETITION POLICY IN THE CZECH AND SLOVAK REPUBLICS

Saul Estrin and Lina Takla[*]

1. Introduction

In this paper, we review the emerging market structures in the Czech and Slovak Federal Republics (CSFR) and the policies to address the problem of domestic monopoly power. Most of the points made in the paper will be relevant to both of the successor states likely to emerge from the CSFR during 1993 in the Czech lands and Slovakia; attention is drawn to the special characteristics of the Slovak republic in Chapter 5. The CSFR is noteworthy because the republics began the transition period relatively late, with most of the mechanisms of central planning intact and with a minuscule private sector. Economic transformation since then has been rapid and the country has considerable potential in both foreign trade and for foreign direct investment. Tensions between competition policy and the desire to achieve rapid privatisation, and to attract significant foreign capital, were apparent from the outset.

When the communists fell from power in Czechoslovakia in 1989, the economy had been stagnating for some years, but in stark contrast to the situation in for example Poland, the macro-economy was broadly in balance (see Begg, 1991; Dyba and Svejnar, 1992; Takla, 1992). Czechoslovakia had been a relatively developed and open economy before the Second World War, as can be seen from Table 3.1. Income per head, though half of that of Germany, was similar to that in Austria and considerably higher than in the other successor states to the Austro-Hungarian empire. This strong relative position was maintained throughout the communist period so in 1988 using purchasing parity,

[*] The authors would like to thank Martin Cave, Lenka Flasarova, Paul Hare and Kimya Kamshad for useful comments and discussion. Any remaining errors are our own. Financial support from the Leverhulme Trust and from the ESRC's East-West Initiative is gratefully acknowledged.

income per head was the highest in the Eastern bloc except for East Germany. It can be seen from Table 3.2 that the CSFR was also a very open economy, though highly integrated into the Soviet bloc. The export and import share in net material product was high with exports concentrated in manufactured goods; trade was focused primarily within the CMEA, especially the Soviet Union. Trade policy is an important element in encouraging competition. Foreign trade was formerly typified by bilateral agreements which rarely took consideration of international prices. During the 1980s, the openness ratio was 60 per cent, roughly akin to the 50–60 per cent of EFTA members and higher than the 40–50 per cent for Greece, Spain and Turkey (World Bank).

Table 3.1 Economic performance of the CSFR 1937; income per head (US$, 1988, Purchasing Power Parity)

	NI/Head
France	265
Germany	340
Austria	190
Czechoslovakia	170
Hungary	120
Poland	100

Source: Various national sources

Table 3.2 Trade patterns in the CSFR, in 1989

Indicator	Percentage
Share of exports in NMP	41.5
Share of imports in NMP	42.1
Share of manufactured goods in exports	47.7
Share of CMEA in exports, of which:	54.9
Former Soviet Union	30.5
Former GDR	6.6
Hungary	4.0
Poland	8.5

Source: World Bank, IMF

The Federal government decided to adopt a 'big bang' approach to economic transformation (see Lipton and Sachs, 1991; Fischer and Gelb, 1991).[1] Most prices and trade regulations were liberalised, and the currency simultaneously was devalued and made internally convertible on 1 January 1991. The authorities embarked on a privatisation programme and numerous legal measures were adopted to assist in the emergence of a private free market economy, with developments and extensions in the Commercial code including bankruptcy legislation (July 1991) and the Competition Law in January 1991.

This chapter is concerned with the role of competition policy in the Czech and Slovak transition process. It illustrates the influence of competition policy in the economic transformation of relatively developed, small and open economies. In the following section, we briefly describe the initial market structure in the CSFR, before outlining institutional and legal developments in section 3. The implementation of competition policy is the subject of the fourth section, and conclusions are drawn in the fifth.

2. Concentration of Czechoslovak industry

Competition policy in the CSFR covers the state as well as the private sector. The public sector is in fact particularly large in Czechoslovakia, even relative to other formerly planned economies. A recent estimate by the CIA (1991) reckoned that state ownership stood at 95 per cent of productive assets of the CSFR, as compared with for example around 60 per cent in Hungary and 70 per cent in Poland.

The industrial structure was developed to facilitate central planning rather than to enhance or to encourage competition. As elsewhere in the communist bloc, the economy was dominated by a few very large companies. The enterprise size distribution for the state sector (which we have noted represents the vast majority of the economy) is reported for 1988 in Figure 3.1. Almost all firms employed more than one thousand workers, and in stark contrast to the size distribution in Western economies, there are virtually no small firms (see Estrin and Petrin, 1991, for a discussion of enterprise size distributions in other socialist economies). The average number of workers, in 1989, in each firm was 3,000 as against approximately 300 in the West. The regional size distributions for 1988 are reported in Figure 3.2; the highly skewed distribution applies to both the Czech and Slovak republics.

To understand how such a market structure emerged and persisted it is necessary to know how supply was controlled by the planning apparatus. An attempt to describe this, which stresses the relationship between the formal mechanisms of planning and the current market structure is contained in the Appendix. The distribution of employment by industrial branch in Central Europe, including CSFR, and the European community is reported in Table 3.3. Czechoslovak employment was disproportionately concentrated on industry and construction, rather than services. This is true not only relative to the European Community average but also in comparison with Poland and Hungary. The share of the economy potentially open to competition by trade is therefore unusually large.

It is widely assumed that most industrial sectors are highly concentrated. The OECD reports that sectors where five-firm concentration

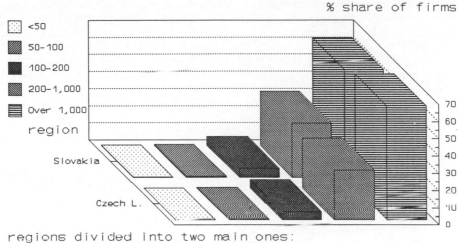

% share of firms

<50
50-100
100-200
200-1,000
Over 1,000

region

Slovakia

Czech L.

regions divided into two main ones:
Czech Lands and Slovakia

Figure 3.1 Firms distributed by region and size, 1988 (1,197 firms in sample)

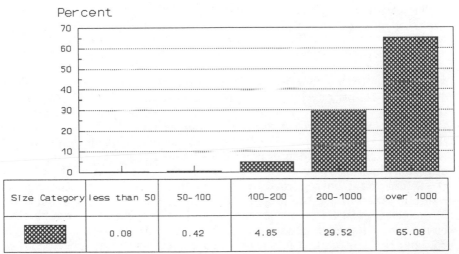

Percent

Size Category	less than 50	50-100	100-200	200-1000	over 1000
	0.08	0.42	4.85	29.52	65.08

Size is divided according to employment levels

Figure 3.2 Size distribution of firms, 1988 (1,197 firms in sample)

exceeds 40 per cent accounted for 48 per cent of production in the CSFR in 1989, and for 39 per cent of employment. In Table 3.4, we outline our own estimates of concentration levels for sixteen CSFR sectors, approximating a two-digit level of aggregation. We report four firm concentration ratios (CR4) by sales and employment, the average level of concentration

Table 3.3 Comparison of economic structure of Central Europe and EC-10 using the distribution of employment by industrial sector (share in percentage)

Industry	CSFR (1988)	Hungary (1988)	Poland (1987)	EC-10 (1986)
Agriculture	11.9	18.8	28.3	8.1
Energy Supply / Mining	2.2	3.3	7.4	1.6
Manufacturing	30.8	27.3	23.2	25.2
Construction	10.3	7.1	7.6	7.5
Services	22.5	26.0	20.7	36.0
Non-Productive Branches*	22.3	17.6	12.9	21.6

Source: National Statistical Handbooks and EUROSTAT
Note: * These are non-profit state organisations in the case of the EC countries.

by sales is 36.9 per cent, and by employment is 36.6 per cent. If we take competitive markets to be those with CR4 (sales) less than 33 per cent, only 50 per cent of Czechoslovak sectors can be regarded as competitive. Even across the republics, the level of concentration is particularly high in a few sectors: tobacco, leather, ceramics and paper. Concentration ratios are surprisingly low in heavy industry, mechanical engineering, electrical engineering and metal working—as well as in textiles, food manufacture and building materials. The rank order of concentration levels is not much affected by whether one uses the sales or employment concentration ratio.

The concentration ratios by republic are even more worrying because, even if the country does not split up, in many cases the republic rather than the federation represents the relevant domestic market. Concentration ratios are typically higher in each individual republic than in the economy as a whole, both using sales or employment measures. The already depressing picture for the federation is not greatly altered by looking at the Czech republic on its own; still only fifty per cent of sectors could be regarded as competitive. However for the Slovak republic taken alone, the proportion drops to less than twenty per cent. Moreover, almost forty-five per cent of sectors in the Slovak republic can be termed monopolistic (four firm sales concentration ratios is in excess of 66.7 per cent) as against less than twenty per cent in the Czech republic and the Federation as a whole. These differences probably stem from the fact that socialist planning was imposed on a reasonably well-developed market system, with a conventional firm size distribution in the Czech republic while the planners created the Slovak industrial structure from scratch to suit their needs as defined in the Appendix. Finally it should be noted that sectoral concentration ratios of this high level of aggregation probably understate true enterprise power in the market place, because fewer firms operate in each market. All of these findings are of course mitigated by the high degree of openness of the economy.

Table 3.4 Four-firm concentration ratios for the Czech and Slovak Federal Republic, the Czech Republic and the Slovak Republic (top four firms' sales or employment as percentage of the industry's total sales or employment)

	Concentration (in %) of Firms Ranked by Sales			Concentration Index (in %) of Firms Ranked by Employment		
	CSFR	CR	SR	CSFR	CR	SR
Agriculture	43.5	66.5	58.8	40.3	65.7	58.8
Chemicals	37.5	44.3	59.0	30.3	36.1	50.1
Mechanical Engineering	19.5	22.5	26.5	21.5	22.1	24.5
Electronic and Electrical Engineering	26.9	24.2	48.8	24.6	24.2	47.3
Building Materials	26.9	22.0	40.0	22.2	11.3	35.9
Woodworking	26.7	29.5	39.7	24.6	26.0	36.5
Metal Working	21.6	16.7	28.5	18.5	12.2	25.9
Paper and Pulp	48.6	71.3	78.4	46.5	68.5	76.7
Glass Ceramics and Porcelain	48.4	47.7	69.0	45.9	42.7	68.2
Textile Industry	21.1	17.6	40.2	19.5	16.4	31.4
Ready-made Clothing	32.6	47.2	67.1	44.5	47.2	67.1
Leather	62.8	74.7	89.5	62.5	70.1	89.5
Printing	40.3	42.2	80.3	34.2	40.5	59.5
Foodstuff	14.8	20.3	27.5	12.4	17.6	18.1
Freezing, Hot Springs and Tobacco	93.3	98.1	100.0	93.3	98.0	100.0
Other Industrial Production	26.5	26.9	82.06	12.7	14.9	75.76

Note: Table compiled using firm data for 1990 (4,333 firms).

3. Competition policy and other institutional developments

Langenfeld and Blitzer (1991) provide a useful definition of competition which delineates the role of competition policy in Western economies:

Competition is economic rivalry in a market in which each seller and buyer independently makes decisions, so that consumers have sufficient choice amongst sellers (or potential sellers) to force the actions of sellers to

1. Effectively limit each other's ability to raise prices above costs for significant periods of time
2. Drive costs to their lowest level
3. Encourage creation and production of goods that buyers demand.

Developments in the CSFR can be assessed against this ideal. Differences stem from the fact that the market structure is so highly concentrated. Czechoslovak policy-makers must therefore decide how to

instil Langenfeld-Blitzer type competition where the majority of enterprises are still under state control. This also raises the question of how to
define the role of competition policy in the privatisation process. The
CSFR's government's position appears to be that competition is a tool –
amongst others – to aid in attaining well-functioning markets. The rules
of the market are still fluid. New firm entry is also difficult because the
credit and banking systems are still not developed. Competition policy
can assist transition and prevent attempts to introduce monopolistic
practices. Privatisation and the restructuring of the wholesale sector are
seen as crucial for a radical shift in market practices. The point often at
issue is the trade-off between competition and growth.

3.1 Legal Developments

The Czechoslovak Federal Assembly adopted the *Competition Protection
Act* (CPA) on 30 January 1991 and it came into force on 1 March 1991. It
applies to economic activity on the soil of the Czech and Slovak republics
as well as to activities taking place abroad which have economic effects
within the territory. The legislation applies equally to public and private
enterprises and to most public utilities. Not covered are state monopolies
that are subject to special laws, like railways and salt and tobacco
manufacturing. Public utilities like gas and electricity are however included. Under the law, a 'dominant' position in a market is assumed to be
achieved by a 30 per cent control of the relevant market. A monopoly is
thus defined in the Act as the absence of substantial competition and a
'dominant' position. Enforcement of the Act is in the hands of the Federal
Office for Economic Competition and two regional competition offices: the
Office of the Czech Republic for Economic Competition and the Slovak
Anti-Monopoly Office. These three offices are independent of the government and can fine entrepreneurs for actions against the Competition
Protection Act up to an amount valued at 5 per cent of the previous year's
sales. The scope of the CPA is conventional and for ease of reference is
summarised in Table 3.5.

For similar reasons, the principal strengths and weaknesses of the
Czech and Slovak competition policy are summarised briefly in Table 3.6.
The Act tackles clearly the issues of creation and maintenance of competition and grants the competition offices additional temporary powers
during transition, to prevent the development of local monopolies by
state and regional officials. The law does not differentiate between agreements amongst competitors and agreements amongst buyers and sellers.
However, an important danger in Czechoslovakia, and Eastern Europe
as a whole, is agreement amongst producers. Managers of enterprises
in socialist economies have traditionally tended to collude rather than
compete due to the peculiarities of the planning system (see the
Appendix). Competition might be better stimulated if the competition
offices had 'the power to negate only those contracts found in clear
violation of the competition law' (Langenfeld and Blitzer, 1991). Another
anomaly of the law is that many sales contracts have to be ratified in

Table 3.5 Scope of the Competition Protection Act

Competition authority	Offices for Economic Competition
Responsible to	Government
Role in privatisation	Must ensure competitive environment
Definition of dominant position	30% of turnover in relevant market
Restriction on mergers	if endangering competition
Anti-competitive practices prohibited	
Price fixing	Yes
Forced contracts	Yes
Exclusive dealing	Yes
Retail price maintenance	Yes
Refusal to supply	Yes
Price discrimination	Yes
Tie-in sales	Yes

advance. This could slow up the other activities of the competition offices, most importantly investigations regarding existing monopolistic behaviour. However, although sales contracts might have to be contested *ex post* if they were deemed anti-competitive, it might be sound to denounce in advance agreements which unequivocally lead to anti-competitive practices.

The Czechoslovak law initially ruled that mergers were not illegal if one of the merging parties had at least 20 per cent of the market. This cut-off level of sales was thought to be too low; the United States follows a similar tough stance against potentially uncompetitive mergers, but the level of sales that activates concern and legal action is substantially higher than 20 per cent. The Czechoslovak law was later modified by raising the threshold to 30 per cent. Although this is consistent with EC law, it might also be too low for an open economy such as that of Czechoslovakia.

US legislation tends to render the majority of horizontal agreements unlawful *per se* as they favour monopolistic pricing. 'Price rigging, bid rigging market division and certain group boycotts' are by definition illegal. Other types of agreements are to be proved unlawful by recourse to a court of law. The Czechoslovak law judges potential cartel arrangements by balancing efficiencies inherent in such arrangements against anti-competitive worries. This approach is not necessarily one which encourages competition and competitiveness in transition. German experience suggests that maintaining competition under such a legislative framework dictates prudence and a powerful strategy when dealing with horizontal restrictions. The EC-German cartel laws, upon which the CPA is based, have a tougher stance than the US, however, with respect to vertical integration. Vertical agreements between a buyer and a seller may be anti-competitive, but their use may improve competition – as an example, distributor agreements which could encourage the entry of new firms into a market. Vertical integration is an important phenomenon in

Table 3.6 The strengths and weaknesses of the Competition Protection Act

Aim	Control of mergers if endangering competition Curtailment of monopoly power
Penalty	A maximum of 5% of the turnover of the last completed financial year or up to the extent of the illegal enrichment
Action	Private action is provided for, based on the US model Any individual can pursue claims through the court system The competition offices can also instigate action
Strength of the Law	*Clarity:* – The law lists 7 elements of illegal cartel contracts. – Mergers are subject to approval if they will result in a dominant market position and contracts that were not ratified *ex ante* are inoperative. – A dominant position when achieved by an enterprise must be reported to the relevant authorities. – During privatisation, privatisation ministries must establish transparent conditions which will ensure that the monopolistic circumstances of the privatised firm will be terminated.
Weaknesses of the Law	– The 30% trigger level for dominance might be too low, especially when applied to sectors where foreign competitors contest the market. – The law fails to distinguish between anti-competitive horizontal and vertical agreements. Vertical agreements are not necessarily anti-competitive. – The fact that three competition offices have been set up – although politically necessary – could lead to 'problems of communication and coordination' (OECD 1991). The Federal Office has sole authority if the pertinent market surpasses 40%. – The monitoring of state subsidies to enterprises is left to the republican offices. Most of these subsidies are likely to be granted at a republican level. Competition policy could thus be harmed through the incentive for each republic to protect its own enterprises. Republican offices could find it hard to prevent 'capture' by republican governments.
Transition Measures	Central and local government agencies are prohibited from supporting anti-competitive behaviour

the CSFR, and in this respect the discretion allowed for in the US law might prove more accommodating in transition.

There may also be problems from operating three separate competition offices. The Federal Agency has immediate jurisdiction over cases where the dispute concerns 40 per cent of a relevant market in both republics. Otherwise, each republic is left to implement the legislation and situations will arise where republics take decisions which could benefit one republic at the expense of the country as a whole. Impasses may arise if all three offices are unable to coordinate their activities and fail to reconcile their goals.

Prices were liberalised in January 1991, and there have been allegations that the subsequent sharp increases were associated with widespread abuse of dominant positions, for example in the food and food processing sectors.[2] There are still some price controls, with regulation based on the November 1990 Price Law. This is relevant to competition policy because it states that price regulation – namely the right to freeze prices for a period of up to six months – will be used everywhere where extensive misuse of prices is encountered. The government will probably only make limited use of the powers given its commitment to reducing its direct control of the economy, but it did take action to moderate price hikes at the outset. Few political concessions have been made to curtail price liberalisation.[3]

Trade was demonopolised with price liberalisation and licensing quotas now play a minor role. Virtually all restrictions on enterprises' current account transactions were removed on 1 January 1991. The annual foreign exchange plan was abandoned, and trade activities by all registered companies (state or private) were freely allowed. Levies and subsidies, which had bridged differences between domestic and international prices, were also abolished on 1 January 1991. It is important to note that foreign trade liberalisation came at the time of the dismantling of the CMEA. The importance of trade reorientation towards Western economies was thus intensified. Table 3.7 offers an illustration of the trade pattern in 1989–91.

Table 3.7 Importance and liberalisation of trade

	1989	1990	1991
Budgetary subsidies for foreign trade as percentage of GDP	1.8	1.2	0
Share of CMEA in exports	54.9	43.5	32.5
Share of developed countries in exports	31.2	42.4	50.9
Share of CMEA in imports	56.1	44.4	43.4
Share of developed countries in imports	31.1	42.6	43.2
Legislation	Trade Liberalisation January 1991 The Joint Venture Act 1990 The Foreign Exchange Act 1990		

Source: IMF, OECD

The process of privatisation is also crucial to the emerging market system. The CSFR[4] is implementing a two-track policy, which consists of a 'small privatisation' and a 'large privatisation'. The 'small privatisation' consists of the auction of stores and service establishments to individuals with the encouragement of small private entrepreneurs, mainly implemented at a 'local' level. It envisages transfer to Czechoslovak citizens in the first instance and only failing that it opens the possibility of acquisition by foreigners. The 'large privatisation' has no such discrimination against foreigners. It aims at manufacturing, banking and insurance organisations which often have a monopolistic character and invariably operate on a large scale. It involves a voucher scheme[5] to put large state enterprises into the hands of private owners. As can be seen in Table 3.8, the impact of these developments on the ownership structure was initially quite modest. At the end of 1990, some 84 per cent of organisations remained in state hands.

Table 3.8 Distribution of firms by organisation type, 1990 (4,333 firms)

Firm	No. in percentage
foreign	1.27
state	83.52
stockholder	2.77
other state	0.44
co-operatives	12.00

The voucher scheme was drafted to satisfy two main objectives: to ensure the rapid transfer of state-owned property to the private sector and to offer the Czechoslovak citizens a stake in the reforms. The programme is being drawn up in liaison with the republican Competition Agencies. Excluded from the impact of the **Large Privatisation Act 27 February 1991** are properties to be restored to former owners by special legislation and all Church property confiscated after 25 February 1948 under the terms of the **Restitution Act 22 February 1991**. Under the privatisation legislation, the transfer of property is first to be privatised to National Property Funds (one each for the Czech republic and the Slovak republic and the federation). The privatisation projects are to be developed by the enterprise itself; Competition Agencies play only a limited role. If the enterprise is too slow, it can be given a time limit by the Supervisory State Agency, described in the Act as the 'founder', usually a ministry responsible for a particular sector of industry. Although drafted by the enterprise, the project is the responsibility of the 'founder'. A bias in favour of privatisation is evident in the fact that the founder has to submit to the ministry also those projects it does not recommend. In addition, property moved to the National Property Fund will not become part of the state budget.

'Small privatisation' has been relatively successful, although perhaps slower than originally forecast. In 1991, the government sold over 15,000 units, with an even greater number having been 'restituted' to original owners. 'Large Privatisation' is a two-stage programme (preparation and implementation), with the second stage having started in 1992. Privatisation is *compulsory* and in the first wave 1,700 enterprises in the Czech Lands and 700 firms in Slovakia had until the end of 1991 to submit business plans to their sponsoring ministries. According to the Czech Minister of Privatisation, an estimated 40 per cent of overall equity being privatised will go to the voucher programme (US$ 6.9 bn worth). In Slovakia, an estimated US$ 3.4 bn worth of equity will be privatised via vouchers. These numbers could change as the privatisation programmes unravel. In the spring and summer of 1992, 1,500 firms are being privatised on the basis of privatisation projects which have been selected from a number of competing projects by the three privatisation agencies.

4. The Implementation and effect of competition policy

It has been a lengthy procedure to ensure the three anti-monopoly offices become operational. The Slovak Republic has had a functioning office since mid-1990; the Czech Republic named the head of its office in June 1990. The Federal Office for Economic Competition began its formal operations in May 1991. All three offices were meant to enforce the anti-monopoly laws from February 1990. In fact, though firms as founders were meant to report monopoly positions by 1 May 1991, the deadline was widely disregarded. The offices had not initiated a single case against enterprises by June 1991.

None the less as we have noted, the government has sought actively to foster the emergence of competitive market structures through its trade, price and privatisation policy. The effects of this policy in the first years of the reform can be seen comparing firm size distributions in 1990 with 1988, in Figure 3.3. It can be seen that for a panel of 898 firms in both years, the population of firms employing more than one thousand workers dropped by more than ten percentage points, and there were more than matching increases in the firm size category 100–200 and especially 200–1,000 employees. The significant restructuring that occurred in the period appears to have had very little effect on the smallest size category. Average firm size in the sample declined from 2,542 workers in 1988 to 2,170 workers in 1990.

The data in Figure 3.3 refers to the sub-sample of 898 firms which can be traced for both years. In fact, the full dataset covers 1,197 firms in 1988 and 4,333 firms in 1990. The size distribution of all these new firms presented in Figure 3.4 suggests that in addition to the impact of restructuring on the largest firms, new entry has been taking place in the smallest size classes. These had risen from 0.5 per cent of all registered firms (private and state) in 1988 to 11.2 per cent in 1990. It can be seen

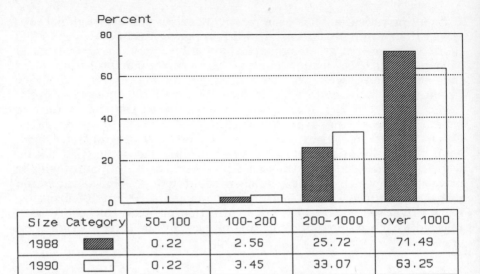

Size is divided according to employment levels
Firm sample is 898 and represents the number
of firms which could be traced from 88 to 90

Figure 3.3 Size distribution of firms in 1988 and 1990

from Figure 3.5 that the changing distribution seems to be more marked in the Czech Lands than in Slovakia. The modal size class in the Czech republic is 200–1,000, but it is still 'more than 1,000 workers', the largest size class, in Slovakia. One might expect that these changes to the size distribution, and therefore to the degree of market competition, might be related to the privatisation. As is made clear in Table 3.8, this cannot be true. Of the 4,333 firms in our sample, only one per cent are private. The vast majority of enterprises in 1990 continued to be in state hands. Hence, despite the institutional weakness of the competition offices at the start of the transition process, the Czech and Slovak authorities were taking the opportunity to restructure firms prior to liberalisation and privatisation.

5. Conclusions

The CSFR has begun to build market institutions and is attempting rapid and widescale privatisation. Competition law looks similar to that enacted elsewhere in Central and Eastern Europe, though complicated by the federal nature of the country. In principle the three anti-monopoly offices have wide-ranging powers to counter the exploitation of monopoly power and to prevent dominant positions from emerging, through, for example, mergers. As in other economies in transition, there are also

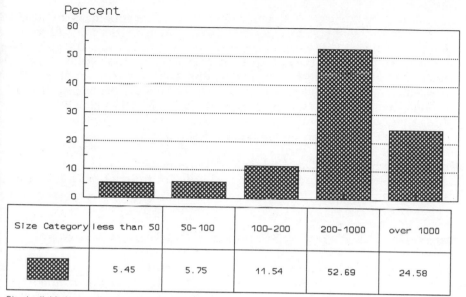

Size Category	less than 50	50-100	100-200	200-1000	over 1000
	5.45	5.75	11.54	52.69	24.58

Size is divided according to employment levels

Figure 3.4 Size distribution of firms in 1990

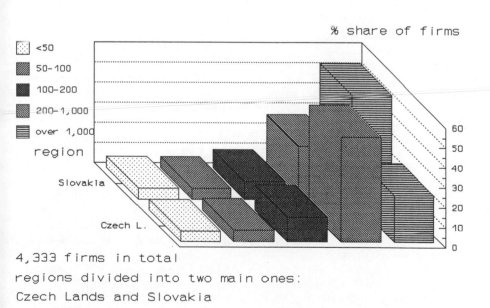

4,333 firms in total

regions divided into two main ones:

Czech Lands and Slovakia

Figure 3.5 Firms distributed by region and size (1990)

agencies deputed to argue for competition in the government structures, for example in the application of price, trade and privatisation policy.

Our data suggest that even in the early days of transition, the government was restructuring the enterprise sector to reduce the average size of firms and to stimulate new entrants. There seems little doubt that this process has continued and accelerated with the voucher privatisation. At the same time, the anti-monopoly offices have been rather slow in establishing themselves, in comparison with Poland and Hungary for example, and appear at this stage to be playing a less significant role. They have certainly not been very visible in the few cases of large-scale foreign direct investment into Czechoslovakia. It remains to be seen whether these offices will begin to fulfil a more significant function once the first stage of privatisation is completed.

Appendix: The Planning System and the Market Structure

This appendix provides a brief overview of the institutional structure of planning, emphasising how today's market structure was determined by the planners. As noted in Table 3.1, Czechoslovakia's market structure was less decentralised and competitive than that of Poland's and Hungary's because planning persisted for a longer time.

Plan targets were detailed, determining the physical quantities that each firm was to produce and the inputs and financial resources which were to be made available to it (see Ellman, 1979). The sole measure of success for the firm was accomplishment of the plan's production targets; profits were secondary. Enterprises were predisposed to hoard scarce raw materials and tended to keep extremely large inventories of final goods, given uncertainties about supplies. Enterprises were large to reduce the administrative costs of the planning apparatus. The planning hierarchy is summed up in Fig 3.6. Enterprise size was also an outcome on the planners' emphasis on the supply of intermediate products and heavy industry, where economies of scale are considerable.

A 'set of measures to improve the system of planned management of the national economy after 1980' was introduced in March 1980. The Industrial Association became the basic unit of production decisions and this usually involved a *horizontal* integration of enterprises into either a 'Koncern' (a large enterprise alone or linked with smaller ones) or a Trust (when enterprises of comparable size were merged). Some enterprises were also vertically integrated into 'Kombinat'. The measures taken in 1980 were far from constituting any type of reform away from planning and few economic benefits. However, they made the already bad market structure even worse.

Tentative reforms also occurred in the late 1980s because of the impact of Gorbachev on Czechoslovakia. In 1987 there was a scheme for 'the comprehensive restructuring of the economic mechanism'; thirty-seven principles for this restructuring were laid out in January 1987 and adopted in December 1987. Experiments began in 1987 with 22 enter-

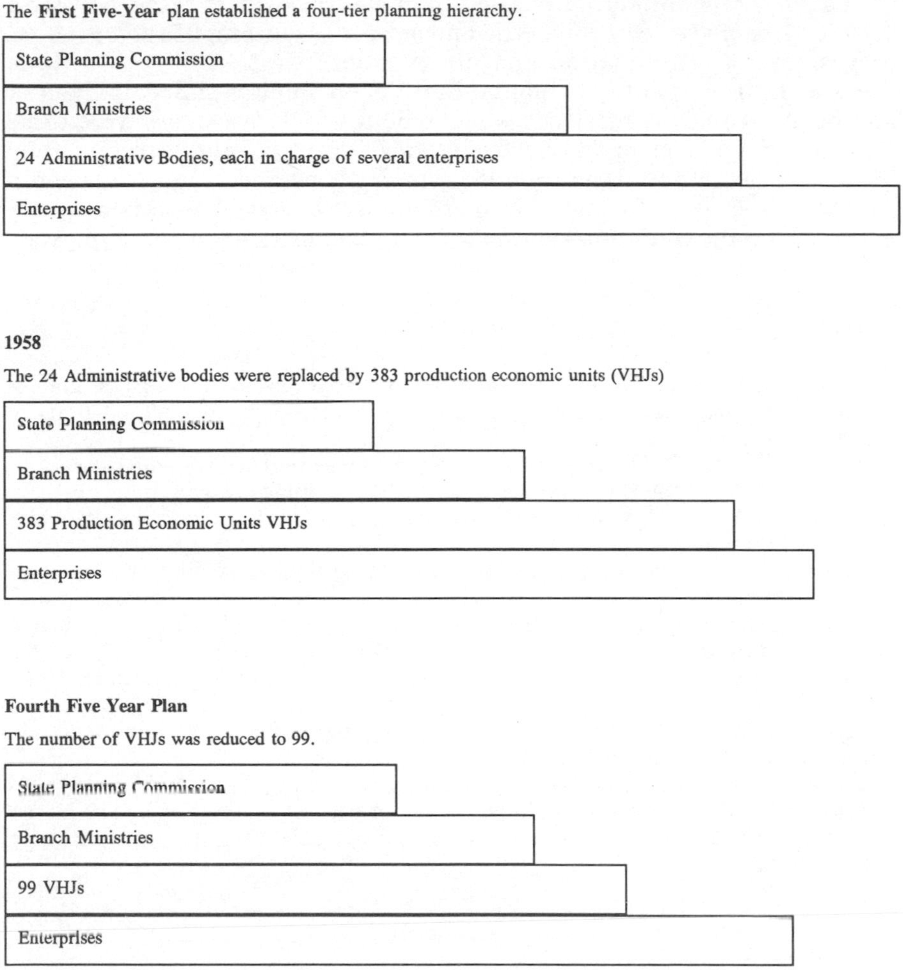

The **First Five-Year** plan established a four-tier planning hierarchy.

State Planning Commission
Branch Ministries
24 Administrative Bodies, each in charge of several enterprises
Enterprises

1958

The 24 Administrative bodies were replaced by 383 production economic units (VHJs)

State Planning Commission
Branch Ministries
383 Production Economic Units VHJs
Enterprises

Fourth Five Year Plan

The number of VHJs was reduced to 99.

State Planning Commission
Branch Ministries
99 VHJs
Enterprises

Figure 3.6 Planning hierarchy

prises which constituted almost 8 per cent of the output of the centrally controlled economy, mostly in the export-oriented consumer goods branches. In January 1988, a further 38 enterprises – or more than 19 per cent of output – were placed under the new system. The experiments involved major decentralisation with firms' economic and technical decisions being made by its management. Ministries were to be confined to investment projects affecting the industrial branch as a whole and faced constraints. They were supposed to, for example, refrain from redistributing profits from successful to less successful enterprises. The Law on State Enterprises was passed in 1988, but not designed to come fully into effect until 1991. It implied reductions in subsidies and for the first time the possibility of liquidation. Liquidation was to be a last resort however; the founding owner was given the opportunity to attempt first a gradual programme of consolidation and direct administration for up to three years with the possibility of merger or division. Managerial, employment and hard currency restrictions were to be relaxed: managers were to be elected and a portion of any hard currency earnings could be retained by the enterprise. From January 1988, small shops and restaurants could also be leased from the state although subject to strict controls on profit margins and the condition that non-family members were not employed.

Notes

1. Unlike in Poland, this was not absolutely necessary for reasons of macro-economic imbalance. The Hungarians, for example, have adopted a more gradual approach to reform, see Hare and Revesz (1992).
2. The percentage of GDP under regulated prices was reduced from 85 per cent in 1990 to 13–16 per cent in January 1991 to 10 per cent or less in June 1991. By October, only 5–6 per cent of prices were regulated, although housing prices are still regulated.
3. The government was worried about the political repercussions in the agricultural sector of the economy – backlash from the strong anti-government agrarian movement. The authorities are prepared to subsidise agricultural produce prices. A special Agricultural Fund, the *Federal Fund for the Regulation of the Agricultural and Food Market*, was unveiled in October 1991. Also household energy and rent increases were initially delayed.
4. A more detailed survey of the Privatisation Programme is available in Takla (1992) and Dyba and Svejnar (1992).
5. There is no proportion of fixed equity which must be set aside for the vouchers programme. However, all equity which is not actually sold must be privatised through the voucher programme. Besides, 3 per cent of equity automatically goes to the restitution fund.

References

Aghevli, B., Borenzstein, E. and van der Willigen, T., 1992, 'Stabilisation and Structural Reform in the Czech and Slovak Federal Republic: First Stage', International Monetary Fund, Occasional Paper Number 92, March.

Begg, D., 1991,'Economic Reform in Czechoslovakia: Should We Believe in Santa Klaus?', *Economic Policy*, October, 243–87.

Dyba, K. and Svejnar, J., 1992, 'Stabilisation and Transition in Czechoslovakia', Cerge Working Paper No. 7, June, Prague.

Ellman, M., 1979, *Socialist Planning*, Cambridge University Press, Cambridge.

Estrin, S. and Petrin, T. 1991, 'Patterns of Entry, Exit, and Merger in Yugoslavia', in P. Geroski and J. Schwalbach (eds), *Entry and Market Contestability, An International Comparison*, Basil Blackwell, Oxford.

Fischer, S. and Gelb, A., 1990, 'Issues in Socialist Economy Reform', WP 565, The World Bank, Washington DC, December.

Hare, P. and Revesz, T. 1992, 'Hungary's Transition to a Market: The Case Against a Big Bang', *Economic Policy*, Vol. 14, April.

Langenfeld, J. and Blitzer, M.W., 1991, 'Is Competition Policy the Last Thing Central and Eastern Europe Need?', *American Journal of International Law and Policy*, Vol. 6, pp. 347–98.

Lipton, D. and Sachs, J., 1991, 'Creating a Market Economy in Eastern Europe: The Case of Poland', Brookings Papers on Economic Activity.

Takla, Lina A., 1992, 'The Czech and Slovak Republics: The Road from Stagnation to Economic Transition', Centre for Economic Performance, London School of Economics, mimeo.

4 COMMENTS ON THE DEVELOPMENT OF COMPETITION POLICY IN THE CSFR

Paul Hare

In order to understand the role of competition policy in the CSFR, it is important to appreciate the economy's starting-point, before the country embarked on its transition to a market-type economy. The key feature of the CSFR economy under central planning was the extreme concentration of production, with one or a few large firms dominating most branches of production. It has been argued (e.g. in Hare, 1990) that there was no need to restructure firms or otherwise break up the large units prior to their privatisation, on the grounds that free entry and exit of firms, together with liberalised trade, should be sufficient. However, undervalued exchange rates, residual protection of some industries, the reluctance of several governments in central and eastern Europe to allow loss-making firms to go bankrupt ensured that reliance on liberalised trade was not enough, and that barriers to entry would persist. Many monopoly positions remained, including in the CSFR, and they were not quickly undermined by new entry or imports.

As Ferenc Vissi of the Hungarian Anti-Monopoly Office has noted, it is not unreasonable to view the economies in transition as underregulated now. They have thrown off the shackles of the former central planning system, but have not yet put in place – or at best have done so only in part – the institutions needed to enable a market economy to function well. In this context, competition policy in the CSFR (and the competition offices at Federal and republic levels) can be seen as helping to establish an appropriate environment for market behaviour, assisting the transition by inhibiting monopoly and promoting competitive behaviour. Even if the competition authorities do not deal with many concrete cases, they help to create a new climate of acceptable market behaviour which economic agents (mainly firms) have to learn and adopt if they wish to prosper.

The CSFR system of competition policy involves three offices: a Federal Office, and offices in each republic. The existence of three offices, with somewhat unclear jurisdictions and overlapping responsibilities, could be an inefficient arrangement, not least because it opens up the possibility that firms' actions which are acceptable in the context of one republic may be damaging to the other. If, as expected, the CSFR splits into two separate states in the near future, the possible conflicts should be less acute. However, this will depend, among other things, on the monetary arrangements adopted in the new republics, in particular, whether they choose to use a single currency.

Given the CSFR's planning traditions, which persisted right up until the collapse of the old system in 1989, it is not surprising to find that collusion among potential competitors is seen as a great danger, with price fixing and market sharing arrangements very likely. This is an important reason for having a clearly defined competition policy, backed up by strong institutions, in order to foster new, more competitive forms of market behaviour. Initially, at least, pricing behaviour of firms is likely to be of more concern to the competition authority than the regulation of industrial structure.

Implementation of competition policy has been very slow at Federal level and in the Czech republic, faster in Slovakia. Consequently, very little happened until several months after the relevant legislation was passed. A common problem, especially in the early stages of implementing the policy, was considered to be the lack of clarity over ownership rights, which could make it very difficult to assign legal responsibility for particular aspects of enterprise behaviour. But in practice this should not have been such a problem, since *de facto* enterprise managers take the main decisions, including those which might be construed as anticompetitive, and hence it is not clear why the competition authority should not be able to act against them directly. A more serious difficulty in implementing competition policy is its potential conflict with the desire to proceed with privatisation. For it is normally easier to privatise a firm which is profitable, while the exercise of competition policy might reduce a firm's profitability by limiting its ability to exploit monopoly power.

We can conclude that competition policy certainly has a part to play in establishing the conditions under which a market economy can flourish. In the CSFR it made a slow start under difficult conditions, not helped by its possible and actual conflicts with other government policies. Its role in privatisation is not yet very clear, though it appears to be expected that there will be some consultation with the competition office(s) prior to agreeing any given privatisation deal. Whether the competition office should have veto powers over such deals is debatable, since this could delay privatisation which may itself be the most effective route towards improving the performance of the economy.

The CSFR procedures also raise a lot of questions about the desirability, feasibility and efficiency of *ex post* versus *ex ante* regulation. The law appears to require prior notification of various deals, to verify that they comply with competition policy norms. But in a rapidly changing economy in which no one is yet very sure what constitutes a 'good' or a 'bad' deal, this is surely very inefficient. It may be better to outlaw certain practices which can be specified clearly, and supplement these rules with some general principles of acceptable market conduct. Then complaints about violations can be dealt with *ex post*, as they arise. In this way, competition policy is not too intrusive, and does not prevent essential change from proceeding as rapidly as it needs to.

Reference

Hare, P.G., 1990, 'Reform of enterprise behaviour in Hungary – from "tutelage" to market', *European Economy*, April.

5 THE DEVELOPMENT OF COMPETITION POLICY IN THE SLOVAK REPUBLIC

Jan Korenovsky and Eugen Jurzyca

1. Introduction

The economy of the Czech and Slovak Federal Republic did not start to be transformed from central planning to a market system until 1990, and prices did not begin to be liberalised until mid-1990, with widespread liberalisation occurring on 1 January 1991. The Federal Assembly adopted the *Competition Protection Act* in January 1991, with enforcement devolved to the Federal Office for Economic Competition for federal issues, and the two republican offices: the Office in Economic Competition of the Czech Republic and the Slovak Anti-Monopoly Department (SAD). This paper covers the experience of the latter over the past two years.

We start by outlining the fundamental problems faced by the Slovak economy in fostering competition. Legal structures and policy development are the subject of the third section, and the work of the Anti-Monopoly Office since its inception is reviewed in the fourth. Conclusions are drawn in the final section.

2. Fundamental issues

Many industries of the Slovak economy are highly concentrated. There were some outright monopolies as well as many cartels when the present economic transformation began. In most cases monopoly power is not a consequence of cost and demand condition, but of administrative decisions by planning authorities in the past. Therefore, the task of anti-monopoly policy in Slovakia is more difficult than in developed market economies.

The situation requires some special measures. But we have sought to ensure that these are in harmony with the basic principles underlying the radical transformation of a centrally planned economy to a market one. The economic issues faced by the Slovak Anti-Monopoly Department can be divided into the following four categories:

1. protection of potential competition;
2. policy towards cartel agreements;
3. policy towards mergers;
4. measures aimed at preventing an abuse of monopoly or dominant position of firms in the market.

1. Protection of potential competition comprises protection of the freedom of entry and the freedom of exit. This enables the market to take care of itself, i.e. it creates the economic environment in which a restriction of competition (and mainly an abuse of market power) sets in motion market forces capable of preventing a continuation of such restrictions.

   Many artificial barriers to entry (i.e. barriers which were not caused by cost and demand conditions) were created in the past by planning decisions of the state authorities. Allocations of markets on a geographical basis or according to a product characteristic such as size is a typical example. This market segmentation is now being abolished. However, it is very important to prevent the emergence of new market agreements made by various trade or manufacturers associations acting in many respects like cartels.

   If a vertically integrated firm has a monopoly or dominant (almost monopoly) position in the upstream/downstream market and there are considerable barriers to entry into this market, it is able to restrict entry into the downstream/upstream market. If it utilises this capability, restructuring, for example splitting it into two or more parts, may become necessary. In some cases, entry is made harder by the ability of a large non-horizontally integrated (state) enterprise to cross-subsidise some of its products or services. This is especially worrisome if the enterprise is a natural monopoly or has its monopoly position guaranteed by the government in one or more spheres of its activity. Also in such cases restructuring to separate off the activities in which it is a natural or state-guaranteed monopoly from the activities in which it is not seems to be appropriate.

2. Policy towards cartel agreements has a wide scope – it deals not only with horizontal, but also with vertical cartels. The Anti-Monopoly Department has to be tough on all horizontal cartel agreements including an agreement on prices or division of markets. This is especially important in the period following price liberalisation. As far as vertical cartels are concerned, one of the main tasks of anti-monopoly policy is to prevent the conclusion and realisation of agreements which give some buyers the exclusive right of purchasing products of the supplier with monopoly or highly dominant position in the market. However, if there are competitive suppliers, possible economic justifications of exclusive dealing (e.g. elimination of the free-rider problem) will be taken into account.

In some cases, mainly in retail trade, large state firms consisting of many units, each capable of functioning separately, act like cartels; decisions on pricing in all units are being made in the headquarters. Such firms should be split into separate units. This can be done in the process of privatisation. Nevertheless, if privatisation does not proceed fast enough, it would be wise to split up such firms into independent new state firms.

3. Since the Slovak economy is still highly concentrated, proposed mergers should be evaluated with care. Therefore, except for some mergers with foreign firms which can significantly increase efficiency of the domestic partner, the policy towards mergers will be a tough one.

4. The best way to prevent abuse of monopoly or dominant position in the market is to ensure freedom of entry and exit. However, if there are high entry barriers to entry which cannot be overcome sufficiently quickly, the Slovak Anti-Monopoly Department has the right to order the firm in question to cease the behaviour classified by it as an abuse of the position in the market.

3. Legislative measures and government policy

The legal position of the Slovak Anti-Monopoly Department is laid out in the Competition Protection Act, though the interpretation of the law has been clarified by two Slovak government statements. The situation has also been affected by the Articles of Association with the European Community, which have ramifications for the conduct of competition policy.

3.1. Competition Protection Act (No. 63/1991 Col. of Law)

The Act specifies the powers of the Slovak Anti-Monopoly Department in the following areas:

- approvals of cartel contracts, mergers and contracts on rights and licences
- investigation of monopoly and dominant position of enterprises
- granting exceptions from bans on cartel agreements and mergers, or their parts, and establishing the conditions for them
- undertaking proceedings to withdraw granted exception if established conditions have not been met or if the reasons for granting exceptions cease to exist
- prohibiting the implementation of contracts, mergers and abuse of dominant or monopoly power
- imposing the duty to remove irregularities

- making decisions whether company's behaviour has the character of abuse of dominant or monopoly power
- issuing preliminary rulings in proceedings begun by the Department
- requesting documentation and information from companies if they are necessary for the conduct of an investigation
- publishing the applications for contract or merger approvals; decisions, in force concerning the contracts and mergers, as well as the abuse of dominant and monopoly power; and information about fines and other remedies.

The Anti-Monopoly Department is empowered to impose fines for violators of the Competition Protection Act, to a level up to 5 per cent of a company's turnover. This is potentially the highest fine in the CSFR legal system.[1]

3.2. Statement of the Slovak Government No. 451/1991 (August 1991) on Improving Competition

This Statement, which was proposed by the SAD, includes measures on improving the competitive environment, demonopolisation and deconcentration. Based on the Statement:

- the Minister of Privatisation has to discuss all proposals of competitive privatisation projects with SAD before approval
- all ministers have to apply principles of demonopolisation and deconcentration during the privatisation process. In the cases where the state-owned enterprise is to be sold directly to foreign investors, either auction or tendering rules must be applied
- all ministers and chairmen of government authorities are required to identify and remove institutional, economic and legal barriers which restrict competition.

The Statement was needed because the protection of competition in CSFR is hard since the market environment is in its infancy. For example, as a heritage of the planning system, CSFR has twice as many enterprises with over 1,000 employees than Italy. The size of these enterprises is usually the consequence of administrative decisions, and the technological and organisational structures for the supply and distribution of goods are poor. The goal of 'autarchy' also implied a relatively closed economy, especially concerning trade relations with the West, and assisted the creation and maintenance of the monopolies. Therefore, the Slovak Anti-Monopoly Department actively tries to influence the privatisation process and restructuring by putting the emphasis on the creation of a competitive environment in the Slovak Republic.

3.3. *Statement of the Slovak Government No. 640/1991 (November 1991) on Public Procurement*

In 1991 the Department dealt with a couple of cases concerning the activities of state and local government authorities. Most of the complaints called for review of the procedures involved in the tenders. The investigation confirmed that, because of the lack of legislation, tendering did not function in an objective way. Therefore, the Department worked out proposals for rules on Public Procurement, which were adopted by the Slovak Government.

The aim of the Statement was to fill the gap which was perceived to have opened between objectives and practice in this area. Based on it, all ministers and chairmen of government authorities have adopted their own directives on how to ensure that the principles of public procurement are enacted within their branches.

3.4. *Euro-Agreement*

The Slovak Anti-Monopoly Department acted as a representative of the CSFR in the preparation of the Euro-Agreement's articles concerning competition policy enforcement between the CSFR and the EC. These articles implied that the Council of Association should accept new rules for the enforcement of competition policy in three years' time. In the interim, the parties concerned will act under their own rules. The Euro-Agreement enables the SAD to take measures after consultation with the Council of Association to eliminate restrictive business practices which could harmfully affect any party. Furthermore, it enables access for companies from CSFR to the Public Procurement procedures in any member state of the EC under the same treatment as enjoyed by the domestic companies.

The CSFR has no own experience in the field of competition rules, so we rely on foreign examples which we try to adapt according to our conditions and circumstances. Further adjustment of our legislation to the EC approach in this area is not possible without further admittance to EC respective rules. That is why it would be useful if we had the opportunity to obtain information concerning the materials of DG 4 of the EC Commission. We appreciate co-operation with developed countries, which help us to solve many problems.

4. Review of the work of the Slovak Anti-Monopoly Department in 1991

The Slovak Anti-Monopoly Department last year dealt with 158 cases, involving more than 300 companies. The sources of the enquiries are summarised in Table 5.1. Most of the proceedings were initiated by the

Table 5.1 Cases in 1991 by Source of Enquiry Initiation

	No. of cases	%
SAD	55	35
Complaint	48	30
Request of the branch Department	38	24
Suggestion for approval	9	6
Suggestion for execution	4	3
Other suggestions	3	2
Request for a law change	1	1
Total	158	101

Department itself. The rest were complaints, calls for review of the entrepreneurs' behaviour or applications for contract or merger approval. A detailed summary can be obtained from the *'Report of the Slovak Anti-Monopoly Department 1991'*. This was the first report published in the Slovak Republic, so SAD was the first government department to provide information on how the taxpayers' money has been spent. Unfortunately this report has not as yet been translated.

The Slovak economy has been significant in comparison to the market economies in its high degree of monopolisation and concentration in production and distribution industries. Despite some splitting up of companies into smaller units during the transformation of enterprises into state-owned joint-stock companies or during the process of small privatisation (the privatisation of retail stores by auction), market structures remain largely unchanged. There remains a shortage of small and medium-sized businesses in our economy, and because of high import tariffs, the threat of foreign competition is not sufficient.

Table 5.2 Cases according to categories, 1991

	No. of Cases	%
Abuse of dominant or monopoly position on the market	79	50
Mergers	51	32
Cartel agreements	12	8
Other	16	10
Total	158	100

This situation resulted in a high rate of 'abuse of dominant position or monopoly power' by entrepreneurs. As can be seen from Table 5.2, a majority of cases considered in 1991 involved the question of abuse. The single biggest case was the abuse of monopoly power by 41 state-owned companies active in regional markets in the purchase and manufacturing of agricultural products. These companies tied the purchase of grain fodder from farms to the acceptance of taking back manufactured feeding

Table 5.3 Outcome of Cases

	No. of Cases	%
Application of decision	62	39
Investigation abandoned	54	34
Expression of opinion	38	24
Remedy measures	4	3
Total	158	100

Table 5.4 Disposal of Cases

	No. of Cases	%
Decision/investigation abandoned or execution ceased because reasons were removed	51	56
Investigation abandoned – unqualified complaint	21	23
Investigation abandoned – submit to other authority	11	12
Investigation abandoned – other reasons	8	9
Total	91	100

mixture. The Department found sufficient evidence concerning the behaviour of 6 companies, and this led to a decision banning such behaviour and the imposition of financial penalties. Insufficient evidence was found for the other companies and the proceedings were stopped; but as a result of the Department's decision, the other companies modified their relations with their customers.

Table 5.5 Mergers

	No. of Cases	%
Approval of the mergers or consonant opinion to the merger which is taken into consideration	41	85
Conditioned approval of the mergers or consonant opinion to the merger which is taken into consideration	2	4
Rejection of merger	5	10
Total	48	99

The approach of the Department in imposing fines derives from the policy of giving companies a certain amount of time to acknowledge competition rules and to comply with them. If violation continues to occur, after this special period, companies are fined with higher penalties.

In another case the Department reviewed the behaviour of the Slovak Gas Industry, a state-owned enterprise, and ruled that there was an abuse of monopoly power. The sole supplier of gas in Slovakia tied its gas supplies to acceptance of conditions which were to the detriment of the customers. The Department put a ban on such behaviour and imposed a fine. During the investigation, it emerged that customers were afraid of punishment by the monopolist if they provided evidence to our authority.

Further information about the Department's record in 1991 can be obtained from Table 5.3 to Table 5.5. Table 5.3 reveals that only 34 per cent of the 158 cases brought in 1991 were abandoned; of the remainder, more than 60 per cent had the decision applied and a further 37 per cent had a decision expressed but not executed. Of 91 cases abandoned or with the decision not executed in Table 5.4, a majority (56 per cent) occurred because the reasons for the complaint had been removed. Only in 23 per cent of cases was the investigation abandoned because the complaint was considered to be unjustified.

In response to the privatisation process, the transformation of state ownership, and entry by the foreign firms, our Department has reviewed many mergers and acquisitions, or their parts. Among them have been several joint ventures. The Department's record on mergers for 1991 is reported in Table 5.5. It can be seen that only 10 per cent of the 48 cases considered were actually rejected.

5. Concluding remarks

There is a lively debate being conducted concerning privatisation, which raises important issues for the SAD. These involve the different approaches of politicians and economists to the question; What should come first – demonopolisation or privatisation?

One group says that an economy which consists of mostly state-owned enterprises cannot create the competitive industrial structures. Therefore, it is necessary to privatise first. Changes towards competitive structures will only occur within the framework of private ownership. They argue that the government had the opportunity to create optimal structures for industry between 1948 and 1989 and failed to do so. Furthermore, the process of restructuring would be slow, and thus privatisation would be postponed, which would have a terrible impact on the whole transformation process in the CSFR.

On the other hand there is a group of experts who say that the authorities responsible for the protection of competition will not be able to change industrial structures after privatisation, because they do not have the power to split up private enterprises. In fact, the authorities do not actually have that power now but they do have the possibility of influencing industrial structures during the process of privatisation.

The range of involvement of the SAD in the process of privatisation can be illustrated by the fact that the Department reviewed and gave opinions on 1,500 privatisation projects in the last six months.

Notes

1. The Slovak Anti-Monopoly Department operates in the Slovak Republic. We can impose fines also in the Czech republic but only theoretically.

6 REGULATION, COMPETITION POLICY AND ECONOMIC GROWTH IN TRANSITION ECONOMIES

Mark E. Schaffer

The purposes of my chapter are, first, to discuss regulation in transition economies in a wider context, meaning comparative economic performance and prospects for economic growth generally. I then want to launch an argument about the importance of competition policy in regulation in the transition economy. The argument is a bit speculative, taking a medium to long-term perspective, but I think it is appropriate. I will be making exclusive reference to Poland, Hungary and Czechoslovakia.

1. The performance of the state sector

These three countries have followed rather different paths of transition. Hungary has seen gradual reform throughout and macro-stability, though the stability seems to be wavering somewhat recently. In Poland, there was a gradual reform in the 1980s which was shattered by macro-economic instability and near hyperinflation in 1989. Reform began in earnest in January 1990 with a 'big bang' price liberalisation introduced simultaneously with a macro-stabilisation. In Czechoslovakia there was macro-stability but no reform worth speaking of in the 1980s. In January 1991 Czechoslovakia engaged in a 'big bang' price liberalisation. What is surprising is that in terms of the basic indicators of economic performance, all three countries find themselves today in about the same place. Industrial output in the state sector is about 60 per cent or so of the pre-reform level; industrial employment is about 70 per cent of the pre-reform level.

Figure 6.1 shows industrial output in all three countries. The timing of the declines is somewhat different – the falls in the CSFR and especially Hungary were somewhat gradual, whereas Poland experienced much of the drop in early 1990, at the time that the stabilisation package was introduced – but the end result is similar. Figure 6.2 shows industrial employment in all three countries. Here the similarities are striking – all three countries have experienced gradual but deep cuts in industrial employment. To summarise, all three countries, despite their different backgrounds and different reform paths, find themselves in more or less the same place in terms of industrial output and employment.

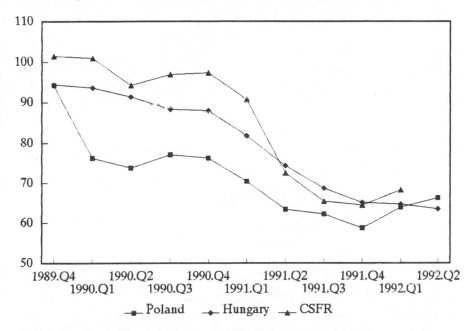

Figure 6.1 Industrial output in the CSFR, Hungary and Poland (Average 1989 = 100. Seasonally adjusted)

A note in passing: we cannot blame the recent falls in industrial output solely on the CMEA trade collapse in 1990/91. In 1991, industrial output fell by 15 per cent or 20 per cent in all three countries, but total exports went down by less in all three countries because the declines in CMEA exports were compensated for by an increase in exports to hard currency countries. In Hungary, the fall in exports by industry was about the same as the fall in domestic sales, and in Poland and Czechoslovakia the fall in exports was much less than the fall in domestic sales.

2. Prospects for the state sector

Here I am rather pessimistic, or at least more pessimistic than some. I do not see any major medium or long-term growth coming from the state sector for the rest of the decade, regardless of the privatisation strategy

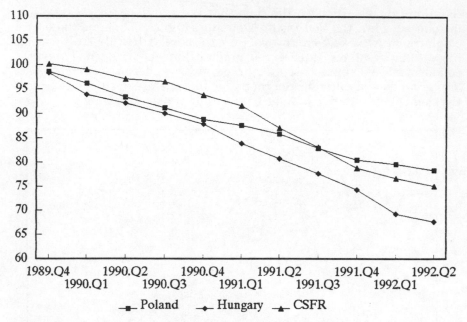

Figure 6.1 Industrial employment in the CSFR, Hungary and Poland (Average 1989 = 100)

used or how quickly privatisation takes place. This is speculation, of course, but the reasoning is this. State-owned enterprises embody a particular type of human capital that developed in a non-market or pseudo-market environment. The personnel in these enterprises lack certain skills, experience and motivations that are suited to a market economy. Managerial skills are lacking and enterprises will find it difficult to form good development strategies. For example, they are lacking in sales skills though in fact they are learning – there is definitely an improvement in the marketing behaviour of state-owned enterprises – but nevertheless it is still poor. Accounting skills and financial management skills are also lacking. I could go on adding to the list but the point is clear. None of these missing skills can be picked up overnight or even over years – the scale of the task of picking them up is just enormous. True, if a firm is taken over by a Western firm it can have these skills implanted fairly quickly. But this option will only occur in a fairly small fraction of firms. Finally, it seems to me rather unlikely that privatisation will make a big difference in enterprise performance, at least in the short run or even in the medium run. Exchanging one absentee owner – the state – for another – e.g. coupon holders – will not be likely to make a very big difference to firm performance. I also do not think that a handful of Polish-type investment funds that become owners of these privatised companies would make much of a difference in terms of enterprise performance. The scale of the task of monitoring the performance of so many firms is too enormous for such newly-founded, and hence inexperienced, institutional investors.

3. The private sector

By the 'private sector' I mean the 'indigenous' or 'emerging' private sector, not the privatised or formerly state-owned sector. There is a big difference. The prospects for the private sector are very different from those of the state sector. We are already starting to see major growth in the private sector, albeit from a rather small base. The pattern is also fairly well known. These are generally very small firms; growth starts in the retail trade, spurred by the privatisation of the retail trade network (shops and the like); now growth is starting to spread to industry. This sector is very dynamic and has the right 'company culture'; it is developing the right skills and so forth. In fact there has been strong growth in the private sector despite the serious recessionary conditions in these countries. In Poland in 1991, growth in the industrial output of the private sector was almost 50 per cent. In Hungary in 1991 output by industrial firms employing fewer than 50 workers (i.e. the small-scale private sector) increased by 50 per cent and now accounts for 6 per cent of production. Rather rapid growth – but nevertheless from a small base. Yet despite this starting-point it may not be long before this private sector comes to dominate the economy. Here is a simple thought experiment. Say we start today with 15 per cent of output in the private sector, which is about right for Hungary and Poland; the rest is accounted for by the state and former state sector. Say further that the private sector grows on average 15 per cent per annum, and output in the state sector does not fall any further. After 15 years the private sector accounts for 60 per cent of industrial output. My suspicion is that this is where expansion is going to come from. Even if the state sector is privatised, these former state-owned firms are not going to grow much or at all unless they are taken over by emerging private or foreign firms. The important thing, of course, is that this growth by the private sector is sustained.

4. Regulation, competition policy and economic growth

Now we come to the most speculative part of the talk, the role of regulation and competition policy. There are two different arguments why competition policy might not be especially important in a transition economy. First there is the view held by some macro-economists that if a country is open enough to foreign trade it does not need competition policy to keep its monopolies behaving properly because they are facing international competition. The second argument is a micro-economist's argument. There have been empirical studies of the welfare costs of oligopolistic behaviour, suggesting that the welfare loss is rather small; that is, the Harberger triangles are just not that big.

Both these arguments miss an important point. If long-run growth is going to come from the emerging private sector then we must ensure that the economic environment is conducive to private sector growth. If we rely on international competition to keep the state sector honest, the private sector is also under fierce pressure from imports right away. It is a very risky strategy to put the private sector under such an immediate strain. The second argument had to do with the welfare costs of monopolistic behaviour. The problem with this argument is that these costs are typically static measures of welfare costs. We are talking about economic growth in a transitional economy, and what is important here is dynamic and not static efficiency. You want to make sure that you get growth from the private sector.

To conclude, the important thing is to ensure that the economic environment is conducive to private sector growth. Relying on international competition as a substitute for domestic competition policy is dangerous and puts a serious burden on the private sector. We should ensure that small but growing private firms do not suffer from anti-competition practices by large state-owned or formerly state-owned competitors. We should also be careful that anti-monopoly policies do not prevent the emergence of large private firms. Competition and regulation policy is not the single key to ensuring private sector growth. Probably investment and credit policies are more important; private firms have to have access to credit at reasonable terms with which they can fund their investment and their growth.

7 SOME ISSUES IN COMPETITION AND COMPETITION POLICY IN TRANSITION

Philippe Aghion

1. Creating competition in the economies in transition

My chapter is addressed to a number of issues concerning how best to encourage competition in transition. Privatisation does not by itself guarantee competitiveness, especially when a few firms have been used to co-operating in a given market. Restructuring may be needed first. But is it better to sell firms as they are and let the private sector do the restructuring, or should the government restructure and then privatise? If the latter, should the most efficient firms be sold first or the less efficient firms? A private firm in a monopolistic situation would not want to split up except under duress. So one reason to restructure before privatisation is that it would be easier to split firms up. The second reason is because financial restructuring is easier while firms are in public hands; it becomes straightforward to get rid of the debt burden because while firms are in state hands, the government is both the debtor and the owner. The money just goes from one pocket to the other.

The second issue is that of trade liberalisation. Jeffrey Sachs argues that you should not worry about demonopolising because if you liberalise trade, foreign competition will do the job. But is this true for Poland? Is it true for Russia? Does it apply to a large country in the same way as for a small one? Several arguments go against Sachs' argument. For example, producers in rich countries who are selling goods for their domestic markets could now price discriminate. They might sell goods of a lower quality to consumers in Eastern countries, or perhaps even not sell at all. For example, if I put a high quality car on sale in Eastern Europe, consumers in France might travel to Eastern Europe and pay the lower price. To avoid this, I will not sell in Eastern Europe or anyway will only sell goods of much lower quality than French consumers would want. Moreover, average incomes in Eastern Europe are much lower than in Western Europe, and producers in Eastern Europe would not buy at

Western prices. Western companies would not necessarily price down all their goods to be accessible to Eastern Europe consumers. It is not clear in such a context of vertical differentiation that trade liberalisation would dramatically increase competition.

Another way to promote a more gradualist point of view on the effect of trade liberalisation is the following 'adjustment cost' argument. You can think of East European economies schematically as having two sectors – a large state sector which is largely obsolete and a private sector, growing at a slow rate because of credit and informational constraints. Suppose you impose complete trade liberalisation straight away. What might happen then is that a large part of the trade of the state sector will shut down, the workers will lose their jobs and unemployment benefits will have to be paid. Unemployment benefits will be financed through taxes, ultimately borne by the new private firms. So if your employment benefits are too large, that will impose a high tax rate on the new firms and then you will discourage entry and therefore competition. In this situation perhaps gradualism is the best way.

Obviously, one must maintain some trade barriers temporarily and the West should accept that. One can think of Eastern European industries trying to learn about marketing techniques or Western know-how as infant industries; you should give them time and tariffs to enable them to catch up. However, the argument in terms of adjustment cost is different from the infant industry argument. For example, in Czechoslovakia it might argued that Skoda is an infant industry and should be protected by tariffs, with Western firms lobbying in the name of infant industries to have tariffs to protect them. You certainly do not want that. The adjustment cost argument implies instead *temporary* tariffs, at a low and uniform rate. They should not be preferential between sectors.

How can you guarantee that they will be temporary? One way may be for East European countries to observe the West removing its own trade barriers. The West has a number of barriers, mainly non-tariff, especially *vis à vis* special sectors like textiles, chemicals, iron and steel and culture. The West should remove these barriers at least, first turning the non-tariffs into tariffs, and in that way perhaps the West can guarantee that tariff barriers in the East will also be temporary because they can say that if you maintain your tariffs then we will re-establish ours.

A third issue concerns other entry barriers. In any country, potential firms face not only natural and strategic but additional entry barriers, especially market incompleteness for example in the capital market, the market for managerial abilities and the input market. Market incompleteness may be particularly harmful both because access to capital market is necessary for someone to start a new firm and because imperfections in the credit market facilitate incumbent firms' predatory behaviour. Capital market incompleteness calls for other solutions, such as joint ventures and franchise agreements, in particular measures which encourage direct foreign investment.

It is also important for financial reform. You would like to privatise state banks or attract new banks because the state banks would tend to give preferential credit to existing state firms and bias against new private business. Market incompleteness increases the scope for collusion that competition offices seek to control. It also facilitates use of a particular agreement for market foreclosure purposes. On the other hand it exacerbates supply uncertainty which could be reduced by vertical integration. A key problem in Eastern European countries is that for example, I would like to sub-contract sewing boots to someone else. How will I enforce this contract? Do I have the legal system which will enforce this type of contract? In the absence of this system, I would be better off integrating with my supplier. Vertical integration can be a positive response to the legal and market loopholes. So competition offices should not be too tough on vertical constraints but be very tough on horizontal ones.

2. The design of institutions

There are problems with regulatory institutions in Eastern Europe. Important examples concern credibility and time consistency, which are exacerbated in transition economies because there is no long-standing reputation to defend. More importantly, there are various constraints on regulators which diminish the enforceability of their decisions. First the regulator may not have the required information to discover breaches in the law. One way to overcome this problem is to allow firms to denounce unfair competition. Second the regulator may not have the means to react to misbehaviour. This calls for a careful design of priorities in the activities of competition authorities at least for a transitional period. For example, the regulator may be more concerned with a clear case of predatory behaviour, than with less clear-cut arrangements. It also implies clear transference rules which can easily identify, for example, regulatory capture. This indicates the use of rules rather than discretion and also argues for independence from political powers.

3. Objectives of privatisation

When ownership rights are distributed to the population at large, for example, shops or the shares of large companies, there will be large numbers of owners. This may cause problems, so you would like to sell some core, because it is important to use privatisation as a source of revenues for the government and also to ensure that the firm is allocated to the most efficient buyers. We know that the best way to guarantee an open competition between the best future owners is auctions. The problem in Eastern Europe is that some people will be cash constrained; competent bidders may have shallow pockets. One way to open up auctions would be to introduce the possibility of loans. For instance, a potential purchaser could make a down payment and then pay the full bidding price out of future profits.

Something else to be avoided in the privatisation process is the use of criteria other than profit, for example, employment as has been used in the former East Germany. If there are several criteria, it is easy for an agency to favour one management group against another so when it believes that one organisational plan will be most able to preserve employment, and if this criterion goes before profit maximisation, it is important that they become the new owners. This is not a good way to proceed; it would be more sensible to encourage competition in the privatisation process. One way would be to deal with employment through active labour market policies or wage subsidies. Germany had proposed such a system using a uniform tax to finance subsidies and in this way maintaining employment or at least curtaining its fall, without biasing the choice of purchasers of firms. The aim should be to keep as market-based as you can and deal with the employment separately from the privatisation process.

8 COMPETITION POLICY IN TRANSITION: THE ISSUES

Kurt Stockmann

Competition policy is not a matter to be looked at in an isolated way. Rules on restrictive agreements and anti-competitive mergers as well as vigorous enforcement of such rules are important, even indispensable in a market economy, but they are not sufficient to guarantee the proper functioning of markets if other government policies are not compatible with the market mechanism. Trade policy, industrial policy, regional policy, and even social policy have also to be in conformity with basic market principles. We all know that governments in market economies often fail sufficiently to respect the two basic rules which they ought to follow in this regard. First, they intervene more often than is justifiable in markets, to the detriment of the economy as a whole and to consumers; such interventions take the form of legislative or administrative measures, or even of government participation in activities that should better be left to the private sector. Second, even if there are sound reasons for intervention, governments often act in a way not compatible with the market mechanism, for example by following protectionist policies or by subsidising large and inefficient enterprises to protect employment, once again to the detriment of the economy and of consumers. My impression is that countries in the West have in recent years become somewhat more conscious of these contradictions, as is illustrated by privatisation and deregulation policies adopted by many states, both of which extend that part of the economy where competition can function normally.

One aspect, however, seems to have received insufficient attention in some countries – the social side of the system. If a substantial part of the population does not regard government policies (for instance reforms in connection with privatisation and deregulation) as socially equitable, this part will feel insecure and unfairly treated. There may be social unrest and that social unrest in turn may become an important factor in the economy. Recent developments in some Latin American countries indicate that neglect of the social side of a country's development may easily endanger the success of economic reforms. Bringing both sides into a workable balance is a delicate but necessary challenge for governments. The good economic performance of a country is certainly one of the preconditions for satisfactory social policies, but the opposite is also true. Unless policies are accepted by the majority of a country's population as socially equitable, there will be no satisfactory economic performance in the long run.

This applies also to countries in Central and Eastern Europe in transition. Governments in Central and Eastern Europe have to do more than introduce and implement anti-trust laws. The challenges they face go far beyond this, and these challenges have to be taken into account in any attempt to identify the basic issues of competition policies in these countries. They have to transform the totalitarian mechanisms, traditions and institutions into those which pluralistic and democratic market economies need. All this raises enormous difficulties of many kinds, most important of which may be psychological. The policies will fail unless the governments of these countries can convince their populations that they are sound and appropriate for establishing a new order in which life will be better, and unless the process of transition takes social concerns duly into account. To formulate and implement competition policies in an environment where there is general insecurity about the future, a great potential for social unrest and little knowledge of how a market economy functions requires much more of an effort than is necessary in established market economies.

Furthermore, competition policies are not a matter of purely national concern any more. We are witnessing the appearance of three economic power centres in the world, one in South-East Asia with Japan in the lead, another in North America with the USA as the leading NAFTA country, and the third in Europe surrounding the European Common Market, soon to be extended in many fields, including competition law, to embrace the European Economic Area. Central and East European countries in transition are already to a lesser or greater extent involved in this process. Within these power centres, convergence of national economic policies, including competition policies, seems to be inevitable, if not desirable, and in Europe this process is clearly under way.

What are the main issues of competition policy countries in transition have to face in this situation? I believe that there are five such issues. First, countries in transition should, if they have not yet done so, introduce adequate and practical substantive rules on competition. Second, they should establish appropriate procedures allowing for swift and effective action. Third, they should provide for the institutional framework necessary for the effective implementation of rules and procedures. Fourth, they should provide the ways and means to ensure that competition aspects are duly taken into account when other government policies are formulated and implemented. Fifth, via their anti-trust authorities, countries in transition should make great efforts to explain the market economy and all its elements, including competition, to the public in general and the emerging business community in particular.

As to the first point, there can be little doubt that from the beginning, when there are still few competitive markets and many markets still dominated by monopolies, a market economy requires the introduction of modern substantive anti-trust rules, i.e. rules that conform to the now uncontested basic principles of today's competition theory and the experience of Western countries. The rules should be practical and simple so that both the administration can effectively enforce them and the emerging business community and the population understand and respect them.

The point raises, however, a number of issues all of which are linked to the fundamental question of what purpose should be served by competition law in a country in transition toward a market economy. The reply to this question is obviously decisive for the content of such law. Traditionally, most anti-trust laws are primarily concerned with protecting actual and potential competition, and this is true even for most of those laws which still use in general, or at least in some areas, broad 'public interest' standards. Other issues like consumer or employment protection, privatisation, or the protection of the environment are in general either outside these laws or play at most a secondary role. Limiting the functions of anti-trust authorities to the area of restrictive business practices appears to be a sound policy for at least three reasons. First, it avoids the risk of tying up resources in administrative activities which are different in nature and often likely to be of lesser importance for the economy as a whole. Second, the more responsibilities an anti-trust authority has, the more difficult it will be to shield it from undue political or interest group pressure which is detrimental to impartial and efficient anti-trust enforcement. Third, anti-trust officials will often lack the expertise necessary to deal competently with other than competition issues. Thus, it seems, on principle, preferable for countries in transition to keep anti-trust law separate from other fields.

A specific issue, however, may be unfair competition. There can be no doubt that countries in transition need legislation against unfair trade practices, a need illustrated by experience of the first phase of price liberalisation and privatisation. In most countries, anti-trust authorities do not enforce unfair trade practices law; enforcement is left either to another authority and/or the private sector. There are some exceptions from this general trend, e.g. the USA, Japan and the United Kingdom; and the competition laws of Hungary and Poland, in contrast to those of the CSFR and Russia, also cover unfair competition. One of the arguments against giving anti-trust authorities responsibility in this area is based on the concern that they may be flooded with cases of little economic and competitive significance and thereby be distracted from more important work. Although this is a valid argument, it may now have somewhat lesser weight because in the absence of a well-functioning and experienced judiciary the anti-trust authority may be the only agency able to protect fair competition at all.

Furthermore, there may also be an argument for giving anti-dumping responsibilities to the anti-trust authority, as anti-dumping policies often have anti-competitive rather than pro-competitive effects – a risk which may be better controllable if enforcement lies with the anti-trust authority.

As to deconcentration and privatisation, there can be no doubt about the need to restructure and privatise the economies of the former socialist countries in Central and Eastern Europe which are highly concentrated both vertically and horizontally. Some of the laws or draft laws of these countries provide competition authorities with sweeping powers in this area. Such rules raise doubts about their practicality, not least because of Germany's experience with the privatisation of the East German economy (see below).

As to the content of a competition law for countries in transition, the basic requirements are fairly obvious. The new laws should have a general prohibition of restrictive agreements between competitors (horizontal agreements) accompanied by effective sanctions. They should furthermore permit effective action against restrictive vertical arrangements when market power is involved. A third set of rules should allow for the effective control of anti-competitive levels of concentrations. Fourth, the laws should make it possible to counteract abusive conduct in a market dominated by buyers or sellers. Simple and easily verifiable rules would have considerable advantages over broad public interest standards for two reasons. First, central rules on restrictive arrangements such as price cartels would be self-executing, as such cartel agreements would be automatically void. Second, such rules would also reduce the risk of undue outside influence on the anti-trust authority, a risk substantially higher if the authority has broad discretionary powers.

Most commentators feel (and I share this view) that emphasis should be on horizontal restrictive arrangements and merger control, while vertical restraints and control over abuses by dominant firms may be, at least in the longer run, of relatively lesser importance. Although there are many legislative options, it appears that as regards restrictive horizontal arrangements, arising by contract or concerted action, the appropriate measure is an outright general prohibition punishable by fines and possibly imprisonment. Such rules would not only correspond to the general trend in Western Europe and in other parts of the world, but also draw on experience in most countries with substantial enforcement practice. Moreover such rules have the advantage of being simpler and certainly more easily enforced than rules for control of abuses which generally require more resource-intensive and time-consuming analysis.

Such rules would also be in conformity with EC law which is not only already of central importance in the Common Market itself, but will soon gain equal status in the European Economic Area. Harmonising national laws with EC law would both facilitate operations of Central and East European firms in the EEA, and encourage West European firms to trade with and to invest in these countries. Furthermore, Central and East European firms and competition authorities could more easily refer for guidance, as regards the application of their national laws, to secondary EC law as well as to EC enforcement practice and decisions of the European Court of Justice. A number of Central and East European countries are already fully aware of this aspect. For example, present work on a revision of the Polish Competition Act, focuses among others on the need to harmonise national law with EC law (see Fornalzcyk, 1992).

One question arising in this context is whether there should be a single rule covering both horizontal and vertical arrangements or whether both forms of restraints should be dealt with separately. As it is generally accepted that the two forms are very different in their competitive effects, most modern anti-trust laws deal separately with them. Where this has not been the case, especially in Western Europe (see the Competition Laws of Italy, 1990, Ireland and Belgium, both 1991), this is explained by the legislators' motivation to harmonise national law with EC law which, like law of the USA, does not make the distinction in the law itself. Although a separate regulation of horizontal and vertical arrangements in the law itself seems in principle preferable in the interest of clarity, alignment with EC law would also justify a single rule on both, provided secondary law and enforcement practice take adequate account of the different competitive effects of such restraints.

As to vertical restraints which often have pro-competitive rather than anti-competive effects, there appear to be two basic options. First, as often recommended, the law could deal with vertical restraints, like many modern anti-trust laws, separately and more leniently, focusing on market power. This solution would have the advantage of greater clarity compared with rules covering both vertical and horizontal arrangements and would not affect such vertical restraints which are pro-competitive. The second option would be not to distinguish in the law itself between horizontal and vertical restraints, like the US and EC laws, but to interpret and enforce the rule according to their different competitive significance. Such an approach, although less clear, would make it possible to introduce a rule generally prohibiting restrictive arrangements using very much the same language as Art. 85 (1) of the EEC Treaty. This option has been chosen by a number of EC Member States in recent years because of the positive side-effects mentioned above, and the advantages may outweigh the disadvantages in most Central and East European countries too. These disadvantages could also be further reduced by appropriate secondary regulation, guidelines etc., clarifying the different actions to be expected in horizontal and vertical cases. The most important issue is that the law must permit effective action against strategies undertaken by dominant enterprises to foreclose markets using vertical restraints.

As to the control of concentration, EC merger control could also serve as a model as far as its substantive standard is concerned – i.e. the test whether the merger or acquisition is likely to create or strengthen a dominant position. A 'substantial lessening of competition' test like the one used in US merger law would certainly also be appropriate. The advantage of aligning substantive merger control standards in Central and East European countries with EC law would once again be considerable for the reasons mentioned above. In this area, harmonisation with

EC law may be even more important than in other fields, especially for the countries which intend to join the Common Market or at least develop closer ties to it. If the rules are different for large and small mergers after EC law becomes applicable because of Association Agreements, or after they eventually join the EC, this might distort competition on national markets and difficulties might arise. Central and East European countries could avoid this potential problem now by adopting substantive merger control standards in harmony with EC law. It is of particular importance that in any case the law defines as clearly as possible what constitutes a merger and that the test to verify whether a dominant position is created or strengthened is practical. Excessive reliance on mathematical standards or rigid market share criteria may lead to unsatisfactory results. Such standards should be used with caution and subject to modifications allowing for a realistic analysis of the competitive situation in a given case. It is most important that the law allows due account to be taken of the presence or absence of barriers to entry.

Lastly, control over abuses by dominant firms appears to be a necessary fourth area of competition law for Central and East European countries.

Because there are still many highly concentrated markets and dominant positions not based on superior efficiency in economies in transition, control of abuses might or even should play a greater role during the transition period than in old market economies. This is a particularly delicate area of anti-trust because it carries the danger that competition authorities might restrain rather than encourage competition, e.g. by overly strict price abuse controls. Hence the field of application of such control should be confined to the strictly necessary, especially in terms of to whom such control applies. This is the more important as there are still many unresolved questions over when market power requires control of abuses. A strict market share criterion such as provided for in Art. 9(2) of the CSFR Competition Act may increase this risk. A high market share does not automatically imply market power, and market power may exist even when the market share is low. Some anti-trust authorities of countries in transition are fully aware of the problems in this area. Thus for example it is the declared policy of the Hungarian anti-trust authority 'not to act as a price authority', a policy not yet fully understood and accepted by the public (Vissi, 1992).

Following the EC model in this area may be particularly advisable for several reasons. West European firms operating in these countries would feel much more comfortable with rules closely resembling or identical with Art. 86 of the EEC Treaty than with extensive provision for control of abuses which they might see as a continuation of traditional governmental restrictions over price and conduct. In addition, competition authorities in these countries could use EC enforcement practice and court decisions which reflect, on the whole, a reasonably cautious interpretation and exercise of abuse control powers. Also Art. 86 of the EEC Treaty seems to be flexible enough to allow reasonable control of abuses in situations at present still very different from the ones predominating in Western countries. All this does not exclude the possibility that in some areas where monopoly situations continue to exist, price regulation may be necessary for a certain period or even permanently.

Even the best substantive rules are of no great use if procedural rules do not allow speedy and effective enforcement. In principle many solutions are conceivable which lie between the traditional negotiating procedure of Scandinavian anti-trust laws and procedures relying heavily on the judiciary, as in the USA for example. For a number of reasons, however, it would seem preferable for Central and East European countries to rely primarily on administrative procedures.

First, it appears that the expertise necessary to deal competently with competition cases is more easily and rapidly acquired by administrative authorities than by regular courts. The fact that the court system is not yet fully developed and functional in most East European countries adds to the weight of this argument. Secondly, relying on administrative procedures and institutions would align countries in transition with the situation predominating in Western Europe. Thirdly, it would allow speedier proceedings if decisions covering the whole range of rules requiring specific implementation were entrusted to an administrative body, leaving to the courts the task of reviewing such decisions on appeal. This would mean that the authority would not only take administrative measures in the narrower sense of the word (for example issuing orders prohibiting anti-competitive mergers or exempting a cartel of small and medium-sized firms from the general ban on restrictive arrangements among competitors), but also impose quasi-criminal sanctions, especially fines. Only where imprisonment was possible would decisions have to be taken by courts.

Experience with administrative enforcement of competition in Western Europe is generally positive, reflecting the advantages mentioned above. The fact that EC proceedings are often not particularly speedy is not a consequence of their administrative nature.

Adequate institutions are as important as appropriate substantive and procedural rules, or possibly even more so. In this context, two trends seem to be worthwhile mentioning which appear to be relevant also for countries in transition.

One of the preconditions for successful enforcement of competition law seems to be the independence of the enforcing authority from political and interest group pressure. The importance of this element is increasingly recognised internationally and numerous new competition laws and amendments to existing laws reflect this trend. If one compares, for example, the first competition laws of Hungary and Poland with the new laws of these countries, one finds that the anti-trust authorities established by the new legislation are much better protected from the type of pressure mentioned although perhaps not fully protected. Many more examples illustrating this trend could be cited from Western Europe, for example France, and some of the Scandinavian countries.

A second trend, although not necessarily of the same weight as the first, which is certainly worth taking into consideration is motivated by similar reflections and experiences. This is the tendency to entrust commissions or committees rather than individuals with ultimate responsibility in decision-making in competition cases. In the experience of some countries, pressurising and capturing decision-makers is more easily prevented if decisions are taken by a panel of three or five rather than by one person.

Another institutional question is whether implementation of the law should be entrusted to one authority only or whether there should be also field offices or independent regional competition authorities. The answer to this question depends on the political structure of a country, for example whether it is a central or a federal state, and on other relevant considerations such as size. Thus, the practicability of or even need for field offices is more obvious in a country like Russia than Estonia.

In the light of experiences in market economies an issue of central importance appears to be the link of competition policy and other governmental policies relating to privatisation, trade, industrial policy, research and development etc. The damage governments can and do cause by inappropriate policies towards competition often dwarfs the effects of private restraints.

In the narrow sense the competitive impact of governmental policies in other areas than competition law and policy is often obvious. There can be little doubt, for example, that it is of greatest importance for domestic markets whether the government follows protectionist or liberal trade policies. In the first case, competitive pressure from imports is reduced or even eliminated, in the second it can exercise a very effective control over powerful domestic producers. Likewise, industrial policies involving heavy subsidies to certain sectors of the economy held to be important for the future of the country may seriously distort competition with substitute products, and disadvantage other sectors. Privatisation may consist, on the one hand, simply in transforming state-owned monopolies to private monopolies, or it may be achieved by breaking up such state monopolies into a number of independent and viable units able to compete with each other.

Conformity of other government policies with the market mechanism is obviously of great importance if emerging market economies in transition are to perform satisfactorily. In principle there are many ways in which competitive concerns of this kind can be taken into account. For example, some of the laws and draft laws in Central and Eastern Europe provide anti-trust authorities with powers to act directly against anti-competitive measures adopted or contemplated by other government bodies. Such rules are, e.g., to be found in Art. 11(3) of the Lithuanian Draft Competition Law and in Art. 2(1) and 14(1) of the Kazakh Draft Competition Law. Although there can be no doubt about the legitimacy of the legislators' motivation and the appropriateness of the aims intended to be achieved by such legislation, there appears so far to be little evidence that such powers have been successfully used or are likely to be successfully used in the future.

Of particular interest in this context is privatisation. There, the picture is mixed and powers of anti-trust authorities vary considerably in

Central and East European countries. The Hungarian Competition Act, for example, provides for participation of the anti-trust authority in privatisation only in the context of merger control, i.e. where privatisation transactions meet the criteria of a market share higher than 30 per cent or sales exceeding 10 billion forint. Vissi, the head of the Hungarian anti-trust authority, finds this participation too limited and thinks that the authority is essentially bypassed by privatisation, a situation criticised in Hungary (Vissi, 1992). By contrast, the Polish Competition Law assigns a far more substantial role in privatisation to the anti-trust authority. Under Art. 12 of the Act, the anti-trust authority may in co-operation with the Minister for Ownership Changes restructure and privatise state enterprises. In 1991, the authority made more than a hundred decisions in this area (Fornalzcyk, 1992).

A more practical alternative to direct executive functions for anti-trust authorities in other policy areas would be a firmly and formally established advisory and consultative role. Such a role would be preferable for a number of reasons. First, it would avoid the risk of overburdening the authority with difficult tasks for which it may not have the necessary resources (for example the Treuhandanstalt, the German authority charged with the privatisation of the East German economy, employs close to 4,000 people, and this number is in no way a consequence of overstaffing). Also, such an approach would avoid politicisation of the authority and thereby reduce the risk of undue political pressure detrimental to its functions. Even if the authority were provided with the instruments necessary to enforce its decisions against other parts of the administration in areas outside competition law, enforcement may raise formidable practical problems. Furthermore, direct involvement may require other than competition issues to be taken into account, and the authority may not have and may be unable to acquire the necessary expertise to do so.

In the light of all this, it seems preferable to establish a right to be involved in all legislative projects and all major policy decisions, in order to present competitive concerns at an appropriate time. As a routine matter, the authority may thus have the right to comment on the competition aspects of any proposed legislation. Thus the Polish anti-trust authority received in 1991 72 proposed laws for comment, and commented on competition aspects of 34 of them. As far as the authority's own field of jurisdiction is concerned, it should of course have the powers to take appropriate action, for example to prevent any privatisation legislation that would be incompatible with competition law.

Transition from central planning to a market economy raises considerable problems of knowledge and understanding. If making profits has been a crime for 70 years, and if making profits is now exactly what is expected from businessmen, this drastic change of fundamental principles and values requires an enormous effort. Large parts of the population will not easily understand what a market economy means, how it functions and what are its preconditions. The emerging class of businessmen will not be familiar with the rules of the game, their meaning and their rationale. Explaining all this will be a primary task for a long time, but it will be of crucial importance in the first phase of transition. Unless the new order is accepted by most and its rules respected, the risk of failure will be very high. One of the institutions best equipped to explain and educate is the anti-trust authority, and it should be an element of its policy to inform the public as comprehensively as possible about its activities, to explain its functions, the rules to be obeyed, the way it interprets these rules and how it intends to apply them. A high profile in the media seems to be imperative both in the interest of a speedy education of the people in general and of the business community in particular. Effective enforcement would be substantially facilitated if the public supported the idea and the institution.

References

Fornalzcyk, Anna, 1992, 'Competition Policy for Economies in Transition', Discussion paper submitted to a CEPR/ECARE seminar on *Competition Policy in Europe*, Brussels, May 1992, p. 1 ff.

Vissi, Ferenc, 1992, 'Dilemma of Formulating and Implementing Competition Policy in Hungary', Discussion paper submitted to a CEPR/ECARE Seminar on *Competition Policy in Europe*, Brussels, May 1992, p. 17.

9 A EUROPEAN PERSPECTIVE ON THE DEVELOPMENT OF COMPETITION POLICY IN TRANSITION

Jean-Patrice de la Laurencie

Three countries in Central Europe – the CSFR, Hungary and Poland – are currently in a transition period before joining the EC. The transitional period is of 10 years, but for the implementation of the EC competition rules it is limited to *three years* – starting from 1992. For this reason the focus of this chapter is on the competition rules of those three countries only; it ignores other European countries which also have interesting competition laws, such as Bulgaria or Rumania.

The chapter begins with a comparison of the provisions of the competition laws of the three countries with the EC legislation. This is a useful starting-point for a discussion of the transitional period, since departures from the EC legislation will in most cases have to be corrected, either by amendment of the national laws or by an EC-oriented interpretation of these laws. Indeed, the Association Agreements state that the harmonisation of each country's legislation to EC norms is a 'major precondition' for its economic integration within the Community. Each country has pledged to use its 'best endeavours' to make its legislation gradually compatible with that of the Community.

Furthermore, the essential provisions of Articles 85, 86 and 92, regarding concerted practices, abuses of dominant position and state aids, are incorporated in the Association Agreements. The Association Council is to adopt rules to implement these provisions within three years.

I do not discuss state aid here as it is specially exempted for 5 years, provided that an annual report on such aid is submitted by the three countries to the EC Commission. But I do discuss the special treatment of public undertakings in Article 90 of the Treaty of Rome, since the Association Agreements provide for its application at the start of the third year of operation of entry into force of the agreement, that is at the beginning of 1994.

1. The objectives and scope of competition laws in the EC and in economies in transition

1.1. *Objectives*

Articles 85 and 86 are the foundation of EC competition law concerning anti-competitive behaviour by enterprises. The former is directed at agreements or concerted practices between two or more enterprises, whereas the latter is aimed at abusive behaviour by monopolies or firms with considerable economic power. These rules aim to achieve three objectives: (1) to prevent the erection of trade barriers consisting of restrictive agreements, and abuse of monopoly power; (2) to preserve effective competition as a foundation for the creation of the single market; and (3) to encourage efficiency and innovation and to lower prices.

The EC competition laws were drafted and are implemented by the Commission and the Court of Justice with the overarching goal of market integration. The new competition laws in Central Europe, by contrast, are primarily aimed at breaking down previous state-owned monopolies and promoting competition to encourage efficiency, higher quality, innovation and lower prices. They reflect the fact that these countries do not face the problem of compartmentalised markets. As a result, their laws do not reflect the sensitivity of EC law to issues related to parallel trade and vertical agreements in distribution and licensing. On this point, they are not very different from the national laws of the present EC Member States.

Another difference, both from the EC legislation and across the three countries, is to be found in the types of practices covered by the legislation. The Treaty of Rome deals only with practices which affect competition on a market, but not at all with bilateral unfair practices.

As is the case in Germany, the Czech and Slovak Federal Republic has chosen to draw a clear distinction between rules governing the maintenance of competitive market structures, and rules governing unfair business practices such as false, misleading or libellous advertisement or interference with contractual relations. The Act of 30 January 1991 'On the Protection of Economic Competition' does not address unfair business practices. They are regulated by recent amendments to the Civil Code.

This is in contrast to the Hungarian Act of 20 November 1990, 'On the Prohibition of Unfair Market Practices', which also covers false advertising, protection of trademarks, fairness of tenders and consumer protection. Finally, the Polish law of 24 February 1990, 'On Counteracting Monopolistic Practices', is directed at 'monopolistic practices', including both abusive behaviour on the market by firms in a monopolistic or dominant position, and restrictive agreements between firms which are neither monopolies nor dominant.

1.2 *Jurisdictional scope*

EC competition law is territorially based: all persons or entities, whether foreign or domestic, are subject to it when they carry out commercial activities within the Community. As was established by the well-known *Woodpulp* decision, EC competition law also applies to non-EC producers who agree outside the Community to implement a restrictive practice within the common market. It is immaterial whether this agreement is implemented directly or indirectly through subsidiaries or agents within the Community. Illegal collusion over sales prices, for example, is implemented in the EC when transactions based on concerted prices are concluded with EC customers.

The three Central European countries have adopted this 'effects theory' more explicitly than the EC. The Czech and Slovak text is the most explicit, as it applies 'to activities and acts that have taken place abroad in so far as the effects of such activities and acts are manifest on the home market'. Agreements restricting economic competition are prohibited by the Hungarian law 'irrespective of whether the agreement was concluded on the territory of the Hungarian Republic or not'. The Polish law covers economic activities 'which have an effect on Polish territory'.

It should also be noted that all three laws anticipated the Association Agreements with the EC by providing for the supremacy of international treaty obligations.

2. *Anti-competitive practices*

2.1 Cartel agreements

Article 85(1) prohibits as incompatible with the common market all agreements between firms which may affect trade between Member States and which have as their object or effect the prevention, restriction or distortion of competition within the common market. The EC Commission is particularly concerned about market-sharing arrangements, boycotts, price-fixing, discriminatory practices, tie-in arrangements and restrictive agreements between manufacturers and their distributors.

Although all three countries employ the same fundamental concepts, each of them uses a different wording. The Polish law only prohibits agreements which are deemed 'monopolistic practices' – which could be understood as practices undertaken by an enterprise with a monopoly or a dominant position in the traditional sense, but which actually include agreements and collusive practices of all kinds. The Czechoslovak treatment of restrictive practices generally follows the EC model, as it provides for a general prohibition against agreements which actually or potentially restrict competition. The Hungarian law also provides for a prohibition of cartel agreements which restrict competition, but seems to limit the prohibition to vertical agreements regarding resale price maintenance, and to exclude other kinds of vertical restraints.

2.2 Abuse of dominance

EC competition law (Article 86 of the Treaty) prohibits abusive behaviour by dominant firms. Dominance itself, however, is not prohibited. The necessary elements for the application of Article 86 are (1) the abusive exploitation of (2) a dominant position in (3) the common market or a substantial part thereof.

In case law, market share is the principal means of assessing dominance: a share below 40 per cent normally precludes a finding that an undertaking is dominant. Other facts must be considered as well, however, including the structure of the market and the ability of a firm to act independently without having to take much account of its competitors, purchasers or suppliers. An abuse occurs when a dominant firm exploits its power to impose discriminatory or unfair trading terms which benefit itself and injure customers and third parties.

On this point, where the Treaty of Rome is rather concise, the three countries' laws have provisions which are fairly detailed. This is mostly positive, but may in some cases introduce divergences in the application of competition rules.

2.2.1 WHAT IS DOMINANCE?

The competition laws of Poland, Hungary, and the Czech and Slovak Federal Republic all prohibit the abuse of dominance rather than dominance itself. The three laws define an undertaking as dominant when its share of the relevant market exceeds 30 per cent. This is clearly the traditional concept of 'dominant position', but with the precise definition which appears in some national legislations, such as the German, but not in Article 86 of the Treaty of Rome.

A more substantial difference appears in the distinction between monopoly and dominant position, in both the Polish and the Czechoslovak laws. Such a distinction does not exist in Article 86, since a monopoly is considered as an obvious example of dominance.

The Hungarian law uses a wider concept than the dominant position by referring to 'economic superiority'. It specifies that this concept covers three different situations: the first is a dominant position with more than 30 per cent market share; while the other two are based on selling or buying power, without reference to any market share. Those two situations appear to be close to the German or French concept of economic dependence, but are not taken into account at the EC level.

A final original feature of the Hungarian law is borrowed from the German competition law. It provides that three firms will be considered dominant if their joint share of a given market exceeds 50 per cent.

2.2.2 THE DEFINITION OF 'ABUSE'

All three laws prohibit a catalogue of behaviour reminiscent of Article 86: market-sharing, price-fixing, the imposition of one-sided contractual terms, an unjustifiable refusal to supply, tie-in obligations, discrimination, and restrictions on production, sales or technological development. Echoing the recent decision of the European Court of Justice in *Akzo*, the Polish law specifically prohibits the setting of prices below the cost of production in order to eliminate competitors. As in the case of the EC model, none of the three laws provides for exemptions from the provisions prohibiting abuse of a dominant position.

2.2.3 THE DEFINITION OF THE RELEVANT MARKET

The competition laws of Hungary and the Czech and Slovak Federal Republic address only cursorily the vital issue of how to define the relevant market in determining the existence of a dominant position. The provisions of EC competition law are very brief on this issue, which has been developed by case law and relies mainly upon the criterion of 'interchangeability' in defining the relevant product market. According to this criterion, products belong to the same market when they are substitutes for one another in terms of their nature, price and intended use. The relevant geographic market is defined as the area in which the competitive conditions applying to the product concerned are the same for all traders. Such conditions may exist in the entire Common Market or in a narrower market if transport costs or other entry barriers exist.

The Czech and Slovak competition law follows the EC model by defining the relevant product market as those products which are 'identical, comparable, or mutually interchangeable'. Although it does not define the relevant geographic market, the tests for allocating jurisdiction over anti-competitive activities to three different regulatory bodies indicate that the Czech Republic and the Slovak Republic may in some cases be considered separate markets.

The Hungarian law states that the relevant product market consists of the goods forming the subject of an agreement and other goods which are substitutes for them in terms of their uses, quality and purpose. The relevant geographic area is the area outside which a consumer cannot procure and a seller cannot market the goods on the same conditions. One of the serious omissions of the Polish law is that it does not address the issues of the relevant product and geographic market.

Once tariff and non-tariff barriers between the Community and the Central European countries are eliminated, the relevant geographic market may be defined on a Community-wide rather than a national basis.

3. Structural approaches to competition

3.1 Merger control

The EC Regulation on Merger Control of 21 December 1989 gives the Commission the power to exercise its jurisdiction over mergers with a 'Community dimension'. Such mergers are subject to prior notification and their implementation may be suspended.

At EC level, thresholds are only defined by turnover. A merger has a Community dimension if the aggregate world-wide turnover of all the firms concerned exceeds ECU 5 billion and the aggregate Community-wide turnover of each of at least two of the firms involved exceeds ECU 250 million. Even if both of the above thresholds are exceeded, however, the merger will not have a Community dimension if *each* of the firms concerned gains more than two-thirds of its total Community-wide revenues within one Member State.

The Commission must only declare a merger with a Community dimension to be incompatible with the Common Market and therefore to be prohibited, if it creates or strengthens a dominant position as a result of which effective competition would be significantly impeded. The question of whether or not a merger is compatible with the Common Market is answered by an analysis of the relevant product and geographic markets and an assessment of the aggregate share of the parties in the affected market. In addition, the Commission takes into account other factors such as the existence of other competitors and barriers to market entry, the extent of vertical or horizontal integration and the stage of development of the markets concerned.

The merger provisions in the competition laws of Poland, Hungary and the Czech and Slovak Federal Republic are rather limited – or even skeletal in the case of Poland, where the law contains only one article on merger control. None of the laws completely defines which types of economic transactions constitute mergers. Following the EC model, the CSFR and Hungarian laws specify that the acquisition of legal or actual control by one undertaking over another constitutes a merger. As a result, mergers include many acts as well as the fusion of two firms: the establishment of a joint venture, the acquisition of shares or the acquisition of assets conferring control. The Hungarian law states that control is 'decisive' when an entrepreneur acquires more than 50 per cent of the shares or voting rights in an entity or when he obtains a right to control the decisions of another entity; this is close to the EC definition of the taking of a 'decisive influence'.

The CSFR and Polish laws do not base the jurisdiction of their competition authorities on particular turnover thresholds as in the EC. The CSFR law states that mergers are subject to prior notification and control if they threaten to limit competition. The Polish law requires prior notification if the merger would give the participating undertakings a dominant position on the relevant market. This is less efficient than clear thresholds.

Prior notification is required by the Hungarian law when the participating undertakings jointly account for over 30 per cent of the goods sold on the relevant market or if their aggregate sales in the previous calendar year exceeded 10 billion forints (or about ECU 100 million). Note, however, the absence of a criterion for market shares in *services* (which could limit the application of the law to products only) or in terms of *purchases* rather than sales.

In addition, it has been asserted that the Hungarian anti-trust authority takes the view that, for the purposes of the competition law, a merger can only occur between Hungarian businesses: the acquisition of a Hungarian enterprise by a foreign company would not apparently fall within the scope of the law. This is rather peculiar, and may deserve an explanation, as it is not the case in any other merger control.

The CSFR law contains a presumption that competition will be restricted and that the merger should therefore be prohibited if the firms involved have an aggregate turnover exceeding 30 per cent of the total market in one of the republics or in the market which they supply regularly. This presumption is rebuttable, however. In its assessment of the merger the competition authorities will balance the economic advantages against the anti-competitive effects. They also have the power to allow the merger on condition that certain contractual provisions are modified to eliminate anti-competitive effects.

A similar balancing exercise between pro and anti-competitive effects is set forth in the Hungarian law: a merger stands a good chance of being cleared if it appears that lower prices, improved product quality, rationalised production and distribution and technological progress will result. As in the EC model, the Hungarian law permits restraints on competition which are 'ancillary' (i.e. directly related and necessary) to the implementation of the merger. The prospects for exempting a concentration from the prohibition is larger in these countries than under EC merger control regulations. It is closer to Article 85(3) of the Treaty of Rome.

3.2 *Public enterprises*

Article 90(1) of the Treaty of Rome recognises that Member States may grant special or exclusive rights to public enterprises. But it confirms that they may do so only provided that these enterprises respect the Treaty rules, especially those concerning competition. Article 90(2), which is addressed to the firms themselves, provides that they are subject to the Treaty rules as long as the application of those rules does not prevent them from carrying out their assigned tasks in the 'general economic interest' (the so-called 'public mission' exception). Finally, Article 90(3) enables the Commission to address appropriate directives or decisions to Member States in order to ensure that public enterprises act in conformity with the Treaty, especially Article 90(1).

The competition laws of the CSFR and Poland address the issue of public enterprises, although in a less complete fashion. The CSFR states sweepingly that public enterprises are not subject to competition rules, even when competition is entirely precluded: the law does not apply to the 'exclusion or limitation of economic competition which ensues from the very nature of the economic activity for which an enterprise has been statutorily established'. By contrast, the Polish law subjects public enterprises to the competition rules: it prohibits monopolistic practices 'unless they are necessary to conduct an economic activity and do not introduce a substantial limitation of competition'. Without any specific indication, it may be assumed that the Hungarian law is also applicable to public enterprises.

3.3 *Privatisation*

One of the central challenges facing all three Central European countries is to manage their privatisation programmes in such a way as to avoid putting previously state-owned sectors of their economies into private hands as monopolies. That is why there are specific provisions in the competition laws of the three countries. The powers granted to the competition authorities to deal with this problem differ in their effectiveness. In Hungary, privatisation is addressed only when it falls within the merger regulation.

The Polish Anti-Monopoly Office has been granted a sweeping power to order the division or liquidation of a state enterprise or co-operative which occupies a dominant position on the market. The CSFR law charges state administration and local government bodies, rather than the competition authorities, with the responsibility of ensuring that the privatisation programme destroys old monopolies and does not create new ones. To this end, the appropriate state ministry must submit an assessment of the competitive impact of each privatisation to the Competition Office in the Republic where the headquarters of the enterprise are located. Although the Competition Office is entitled to give its opinion, the Republican Government will have the final say in the case of a conflict of opinion. Local government bodies responsible for the privatisation of services in regional and local markets are also charged with ensuring that the enterprises under their responsibility do not create or maintain monopolies or dominant positions when they enter the private sector.

A foreign investor purchasing or acquiring a controlling stake in a company in the CSFR may find itself in a monopolistic or dominant position in a particular product market. The competition authorities may then intervene to split up the company and force a sale of some of its parts. Sometimes, however, anti-trust concerns bow to economic and political necessities. The acquisition by Volkswagen of a controlling interest in Skoda is a good example of this. Despite the resulting monopoly of Volkswagen in the CSFR automobile market, the competition authorities did not object. One may conclude that there was considerable political pressure for the deal to go through. One possible legal basis for approval may be found in the interim provisions relating to privatisation: in making their assessment of the compatibility of a privatisation with the competition law, the relevant state bodies may take account of foreign competition likely to arise in the home market over the next two years. The rapid reduction in the tariffs, subsidies and quotas protecting Czechoslovak industry from world competition may have led to the conclusion that Skoda would rapidly lose market share.

4. Methods of enforcement

4.1 Regulatory philosophy

4.1.1 IS NOTIFICATION COMPULSORY OR NOT?

The EC Commission enjoys exclusive authority to grant individual exemptions and negative clearances and to issue block exemption regulations. While firms are not obliged to notify their agreements to the Commission, they often do so in order to claim an individual exemption under Article 85(3) and, in any event, to gain immunity from fines during the post-notification period.

An agreement may be granted an individual exemption or fall within one of the block exemption regulations. As a general rule, the Commission has been willing to grant individual exemptions and establish block exemptions for co-operative agreements involving rationalisation or modernisation of production or distribution, a reduction in costs and an increase in production capacity. In deciding whether to grant an exemption the Commission examines whether consumers are assured a fair share of the resulting benefits and whether the restrictions of competition in the agreement are indispensable.

Of the Central European states, the regulatory regime set up by the CSFR law creates by far the greatest administrative burden. All agreements which have a restrictive effect on trade must be submitted to the Federal Office for Economic Competition for entry into a 'cartel register'. They are impermissible and void unless the law specifically provides otherwise or the Office grants an exemption. Even agreements which are not prohibited outright – such as agreements which rationalise production, apply commercial discounts and have a *de minimis* impact on competition – must be approved by the Office in order to be valid. Restrictive practices may be exempted for a certain period if the limitations on competition which they cause are essential to the promotion of technical and economic development.

This system of mandatory notification based on the presumption of illegality will be certain to generate a backlog of cases, lengthy review proceedings and an overwhelming need for qualified civil servants. It is made somewhat more flexible, however, by a provision similar to the non-opposition procedure in the EC block exemption regulations: a notified agreement becomes valid if the Federal Office for Economic Competition does not register its objection within three months of notification.

4.1.2 *'DE MINIMIS'*

In the EC, agreements which do not restrict competition to an appreciable extent need not be notified. According to the Commission's *de minimis* rule, agreements do not fall within Article 85(1) if the goods and services covered by them do not represent more than 5 per cent of the total market for goods and services in the Community and if the aggregate annual turnover of the participating undertakings does not exceed ECU 200 million.

The competition laws of the CSFR and Hungary provide for individual exemptions and *de minimis* rules like those of the EC. In the CSFR, agreements which impose uniform trading, supply or payment conditions, or which have a market share of less than five per cent of the national market or less than 30 per cent of a local market, are considered to pose a marginal threat to competition. Such agreements may be exempted by application to the competent anti-trust authority. The applicant must show that the limitation on competition is essential for the public interest and would promote technical and economic development. The Hungarian law treats restrictions on competition as *de minimis* and therefore permissible if the joint share of the contracting parties for the goods subject to the agreement does not exceed 10 per cent of the market in a given geographic area.

The Polish law does not adopt a specific test defining agreements of minor importance. Rather, it states that restrictive agreements will not be prohibited if they 'are necessary to conduct an economic activity and do not induce a substantial limitation on competition'.

4.1.3 EXEMPTIONS

The laws of the Central European states provide for a procedure by which restrictive agreements may be exempted upon application to the competition authorities. The Polish Anti-Monopoly Office is likely to exempt any arrangement which lowers production or sales costs or improves product quality without leading to 'a significant restriction of competition or conditions for its emergence on a given market'.

There is a remarkable provision in the Hungarian law: an anti-competitive agreement is not prohibited if 'it is aimed at stopping abuse of economic superiority'. A similar provision does not exist in the EC, or, to my knowledge, in any developed country. In my view, it is too dangerous; the appropriate way to defend oneself is to lodge a complaint before the courts and/or the competition authorities.

None of the three countries' legislation on cartel agreements provides for block exemptions for certain types of co-operation between undertakings. However, the Czechoslovak law provides a list of possible cases, particularly rationalisation or licence agreements, for which an *a priori* exemption can be obtained by firms, if they apply for it.

4.2 Competition authorities

The effectiveness of an anti-trust enforcement policy hinges on the independence of the responsible authority and the powers at its disposal to obtain information and impose penalties for non- compliance. The reality of this independence is rather delicate and difficult to estimate.

EC competition rules are implemented primarily by the Commission, in particular by the Directorate-General for Competition and the Legal Service. The members of the Commission are nominated by the Member States but remain independent. The officials of the Commission who help shape competition policy are not bound by contractual, financial or political ties to the governments of their Member States. This explains to a large extent why the Commission can be considered as a truly independent executive body.

By contrast, the competition authorities of the Central European states are part of, and subject to, their respective governments. Although there is insufficient evidence to date to form a definitive judgement, there is a concern that these authorities will lack the power to make and enforce politically unpopular decisions.

The competition laws of Poland and Hungary are implemented by an Anti-Monopoly Office and an Office of Economic Competition, respectively. Although these bodies also enjoy broad supervisory and investigatory powers, they may lack the independence to be fully effective.

As in many Western countries, the competition authorities are appointed by the government. The Polish Anti-Monopoly Office is subordinated to the Council of Ministers and its president can be removed by the prime minister. However, being a member of the Council of Ministers gives the president of this Office an important informal power. The president of the Hungarian Office of Economic Competition can also be removed by the president of the Republic upon the proposal of the prime minister but only for extremely serious reasons.

In the CSFR, the competition authorities depend more on the government but our concern is rather the consequence of the separate jurisdictions of the three competition offices. While the Offices in the two republics handle cases having anti-competitive effects primarily in their respective republics, the Federal Office is charged with cases involving an actual or potential market share exceeding 40 per cent in each republic. If the Federation dissolves, revisions will be necessary.

4.3 Enforcement powers

In the EC, Member States and any natural or legal person claiming a legitimate interest may file a complaint with the Commission. Although most infringement cases are opened after a complaint is lodged by a third party, the Commission occasionally institutes proceedings on its own initiative. It enjoys considerable discretion in its choice of which infringement complaints to review: it may refuse to pursue infringements brought to its attention and may decide to settle a case without adopting any formal decision or imposing a fine.

The Commission enjoys various powers such as the power to request companies to disclose information or to conduct on-site investigations. Although the provisions of EC Regulation 17/62 were not entirely clear in this respect, the Court of Justice has confirmed, in the *Hoechst* case, that the Commission has powers of compulsory search and may take actual possession of documents, subject to the prior authority of the National Court which has territorial jurisdiction. In cases of infringement, the Commission may adopt a reasoned decision which may be appealed to the Court of First Instance and the Court of Justice. It can also impose fines where appropriate (up to 10 per cent of turnover) or take interim measures when they are urgent.

The scope of enforcement powers entrusted to the three competition authorities in the CSFR appears, on paper at least, to be as considerable as those granted to the Commission. They, too, may inspect legal and commercial documents, request explanations on the spot, take interim measures, issue decisions requiring the cessation of anti-competitive practices and fix fines for infringement. The Hungarian law is rather more expansive than the other two in this regard: it specifically allows the investigator to 'enter any room of the examined entrepreneur' and to 'seek information from any of his employees orally or in written form'. In addition, in certain cases, the Hungarian authorities have the express power to impound documents. It is less clear whether investigation powers in the other countries extend to actual seizure of documents. In any event, none of the Central European laws examined appears to provide for prior authorisation or *a posteriori* control by the Courts of the exercise by the competition authorities of their investigative powers. Finally, in Hungary and Poland, the competition authorities have the unusual power to issue a decision compelling an infringing party to lower its prices.

Following an investigation started at the request of interested parties or on the initiative of the offices charged with implementing the competition laws in the Central European states, abuses of dominant position may either be prohibited or subject to a fine. In Poland this fine amounts to up to 15 per cent of the revenue of the infringing undertaking in its last financial year. The competition offices in the CSFR have the power to impose fines of up to 5 per cent of the infringing undertaking's turnover. In Hungary the fine must exceed by at least 30 per cent but cannot be more than double the profit gained by the undertaking by means of its unlawful conduct. This is a more American than European way of sanctioning anti-competitive practices, but we must wait for the results before making any judgement.

4.4 Administrative procedures

Procedural rights are scrupulously respected by the EC competition rules. These rights are enshrined above all in Regulation 17/62. Before the Commission adopts a decision, it must first send the parties a 'Statement of Objections' which recites the facts and legal reasoning leading the Commission to believe that an infringement has occurred. Once the parties have submitted their written comments, they may request an oral hearing at which they will be represented by counsel. Interested third parties may also request to be heard. Only after this procedure has been completed may the Commission reach a decision that Article 85 or 86 has been infringed and issue orders that the infringement should be brought to an end, and/or impose fines.

None of the competition laws of the Central European states treats procedural rights at length. This must be partly due to the fact that these rights are dealt with separately in laws relating to administrative procedure or in the Civil Code of each state. However, none of them ignores the issue completely.

The three laws provide that administrative proceedings are opened either on the initiative of the competition authorities or following the lodging of a complaint. Only an interested person may file a complaint. State bodies and public consumer protection groups qualify as interested parties. The Hungarian law allows an interested party to file a court action rather than to lodge a complaint with the Office of Economic Competition. In its court action the party may ask for an injunction, the restoration of the *status quo ante* and/or damages. The limitation period within which a court action must be brought is six months from the day the infringement was discovered or three years from the date of the infringement itself, whichever is the later.

The three laws provide that hearings shall be attended by parties directly interested in the case and that persons or associations of persons may request to be present if their interests may be affected by the decision of the competition authority. The Hungarian law, however, goes a step further by explicitly granting the defence the right to inspect the documents serving as the basis for the investigation. Final decisions of the competition authorities may be appealed to a court of competent jurisdiction.

5. Conclusion

It is still too early to make definitive judgements about the effectiveness of the competition laws in the Central European States. The comparison above is only a quick overview, and many points have to be more thoroughly analysed and qualified, while others of possible relevance have not even been mentioned.

An assessment, however, may be advanced concerning the compatibility of these laws with the competition rules of the EC. All three laws incorporate the major elements of the Community's competition rules. As their economies mature and as the process of integration with Western Europe continues, the focus of their laws should shift from abuses of monopolies or dominant positions to restrictive practices.

It is obvious that the laws are most detailed on the concept of dominance, which is not incompatible with the EC legislation. But some specific limitations in the scope of the competition law such as provisions which allow practices forbidden in the EC will have to be abandoned, by a modification of the statutes or by case law.

From a more practical standpoint, the lengthy backlog of cases facing the Directorate-General for Competition and the vast resources in terms of both time and money required to grant exemptions in Brussels should convince the Central European States to avoid overly bureaucratic mechanisms. They may wish to consider the advantages of reducing the need for exemptions by adopting a rule of reason analysis or by establishing clear regulations for block exemptions.

Overall, the three laws we have examined are very close to those of many Western European countries. Limited adjustments may be necessary to the laws themselves, but the most important adjustments are in the harmonisation of enforcement with EC rules. This has to be done progressively, on the basis of continuous comparisons, and is a task for the Association Council and for each national authority. It is mainly through such reciprocal exchanges of experience and mutual training (through the OECD and EC meetings) that Western European countries have developed and improved their competition policy.

10 RESTRUCTURING FOR COMPETITION

Sally J. Van Siclen[*]

1. Introduction

Many countries are today attempting to transform their economies. Until recently these economies were characterised by central planning, widespread state ownership of property and structures that were the products of political rather than economic forces. Now, these countries are seeking to create market-driven economies with widespread private property. The prerequisites for successful transformation include constructing an appropriate legal infrastructure, introducing an accounting system and capital markets, reducing barriers to international trade, making the currency convertible and privatising property. Without breaking apart monopolies, however, these changes would be ineffective: monopolies produce inefficiently low output, stifle competition through the control of scarce resources and impede improvements in production techniques. This paper focuses on demonopolisation.

Demonopolisation, as the term is used here, means the breaking apart of one enterprise into several separately owned and managed enterprises. This 'breaking apart' may entail both horizontal and vertical fissuring. The goal of demonopolisation is the creation of competing enterprises, so that products are supplied at competitive (more efficient) prices, quantities and qualities, rather than at monopoly or regulated levels. Demonopolisation may also create markets that do not currently exist, so that intermediate products become available to new enterprises for use as inputs into downstream products. Rational demonopolisation is not a formulaic dismemberment of an existing monopoly; it is the separation of productive assets of a monopoly into efficiently configured groups of

* Competition and Consumer Policy Division, OECD. The views expressed herein do not necessarily represent those of the OECD. Thanks to Jonathan Baker, William Gillespie, Janusz Ordover, Marilyn Simon, Gregory Werden, and the editors of the current volume, for their useful comments on earlier drafts. All errors are my own.

assets so that the resulting daughter enterprises face competitors and are profitable both in the long term and short term. Demonopolisation is a short cut, an attempt to create quickly relatively efficient enterprise and market structures, structures that otherwise might result only from years of competition in a market economy.

These demonopolisation policy comments are based upon a central tenet of neoclassical economics: in an appropriate legal environment, enterprises that supply competitive markets operate more efficiently and serve consumers better than monopolies. Further, monopolies that result from central planning are likely to be less efficient than monopolies that arise in a market economy. Given a policy decision to demonopolise, however, the choices among the various possible market structures, especially deciding how many daughter enterprises to create, are more difficult to make and depend upon the facts of the particular market. This chapter suggests an approach to making these demonopolisation choices.

Each enterprise requires a unique analysis for demonopolisation. Although demonopolisation is an important tool for creating more competitive market structures, it may be unnecessary for some enterprises. In some markets, for example, barriers to international trade or to entry by new enterprises may be sufficiently low that foreign or new suppliers will compete effectively against the incumbent enterprise, even if it is not demonopolised. In other markets, import or other barriers may protect a monopoly and demonopolisation may create inefficient enterprises. In these latter cases, potentially superior alternatives to demonopolisation include: the privatisation and subsequent regulation of the monopoly; the retention of state ownership, with or without state management; and the privatisation of the monopoly and later reduction of barriers to new competition.

In still other cases, the benefits of demonopolisation may be obvious and the partition easy. For example, truck transportation is easily demonopolised in the privatisation process by selling the vehicles to separate owners. Demonopolisation of most retail establishments and service businesses is similarly easily accomplished, if their input markets are functioning well.

The focus of this chapter is the demonopolisation of enterprises that are neither in industries for which demonopolisation is clearly unnecessary or undesirable, nor in industries for which demonopolisation is clearly desirable and the partition is obvious.

1.1 Demonopolisation and privatisation

Demonopolisation is a part of the privatisation process. Privatisation of state monopolies without demonopolisation has limited benefits. It may provide monopolies with incentives to minimise costs given input prices. However, such privatisation would not, in general, result in efficient choices of outputs because private monopolies generally choose to produce less than would be socially optimal. Further, in an economy crowded with monopolists, the prices of many intermediate products will be distorted from their competitive levels. Distorted prices provide incentives for the inefficient use of those products. The privatisation of monopolies is superficially attractive because it may increase the revenues realised by government from the sale of state assets. Buyers generally will pay more for productive assets held by a monopoly than they will pay, in the aggregate, for the same assets held by competitive firms. But the revenue increase may not compensate for the social welfare loss caused by monopoly, even if raising state revenues by other means causes other distortions.

1.2 The present chapter

Demonopolisation involves choosing among a wide array of possible enterprise and market structures throughout an economy with radically changing prices and legal infrastructure. Admittedly, with finite time and resources, neither the optimal enterprise size nor the best market structure will be found. The purpose of this chapter is to identify readily applied methods for demonopolisation that do not fail too badly too often. It applies to some of the problems of demonopolisation some of the methodology used to evaluate mergers in the United States – notably the concept of relevant markets – and some basic concepts of industrial organisation economics, especially economies of scale and scope, vertical integration and effects of market entry.

Given a decision to demonopolise, the demonopolisation approach presented here begins with an examination of the relationships among the current assets of a given state monopolist. Some assets should be held within a single enterprise in order to exploit economies of scale or scope or to exploit efficiencies of vertical integration. Other currently intra-enterprise relationships can be replaced, without significant efficiency loss, by arms' length transactions in a market.

Once these relationships are understood, the decisions about which assets belong together in one enterprise and which must be assigned to separate enterprises can be made. Sometimes the benefits of additional competitors must be balanced against the benefits of economies of scale and vertical integration. The trade-off between efficiencies from vertical integration and the efficiencies resulting from creating formerly missing markets may also be weighed. After the partitioning decisions have been made, the new market structures are evaluated.

Section 2 of this chapter discusses the decision whether to demonopolise. This includes an examination of how international trade, foreign competitors and entry into markets can limit anti-competitive behaviour. Section 3 addresses the partition of a monopoly enterprise, that is, how the nature of the relationships among assets determines whether those assets should remain in the same enterprise or be split among separate enterprises. Section 4 is an overview of the evaluation of competition resulting from demonopolisation. An example of demonopolisation of a retailing monopolist is worked through (Section 5). A conclusion follows in Section 6. Because the concept of a market is central to effective demonopolisation, the Appendix discusses the definition of relevant product and geographic markets and provides a method for their approximate delineation in economies where prices are unpredictable.

2. Whether to demonopolise

The first demonopolisation decision is whether to do it at all. Demonopolisation may be unnecessary for some enterprises. The level of competition may not be increased by breaking apart incumbent monopolies that face effective competition from foreign suppliers or from new entrants. Other monopolies, protected from competition, may have sufficiently large economies of scale given the size of the domestic markets that demonopolisation would result in enterprises with substantially higher production costs than the monopolies. In these cases, alternatives to demonopolisation should be considered.

2.1 Markets with international trade

International trade may limit the effect that demonopolisation of domestic industry has on competitive behaviour in a market. If there are low transportation costs and low import barriers so that foreign producers are effective competitors of domestic producers, then demonopolisation will not significantly improve the competitive performance of that market.

Barriers to international trade can take various forms. Import barriers include not only tariffs and quotas; certain laws can aid or hinder international trade. For example, foreign sellers usually insist upon a convertible currency and the right to repatriate profits as prerequisites for trade. Foreign producers of a good that requires a distribution system, perhaps to provide technical service, need a contract law and the supporting legal system to ensure that they can make enforceable contracts with local distributors. Foreign investment laws can prohibit foreign ownership of certain production plants or protect property from confiscation. Foreign licensors are less likely to license domestic producers if an intellectual property law insufficiently protects licensors' intellectual property. If these laws are inadequate, then competition from foreign producers may not be sufficient to prevent anti-competitive conduct by domestic monopolies.

'Temporary protectionism' which countries undergoing radical economic change may find attractive in order to, for example, preserve the current pattern of employment, affects the decision to demonopolise. Temporary monopoly prices may distort decisions regarding investments that will last beyond the period of protection. For example, a temporarily protected monopoly may invest in high-cost capacity, with which it will be encumbered long after the removal of tariff barriers. When long-term distortions would be large, it might be advisable to demonopolise an enterprise supplying markets for internationally tradable products even if import barriers were expected to be temporary. Demonopolisation would be inadvisable, however, if the long-term negative effects of mono-poly were small and the import barriers were truly short-lived. In this case, the benefits of demonopolisation would be limited to those derived during the period of protection and therefore would be small.

When import barriers and transportation costs are low, foreign sup-pliers can compete against domestic enterprises. If foreign suppliers provide sufficient competition for domestic producers of a good, then demonopolising the domestic assets that supply that market would gen-erally not increase the level of competition in that market. Other mar-kets supplied by other assets held in the same state enterprise might still benefit from demonopolisation however. When import barriers are low, the following products, for example, might be tradable: various sorts of steel, trucks and automobiles, large electrical generation and distri-bution equipment, some chemicals and many other manufactured or other agricultural products. However, if a product is not tradable or if there exist other barriers to free importation, then demonopolisation may be advisable because enterprises that sell these products are less likely to face effective competition from foreign producers. For example, retail products, distribution and professional services are not usually traded internationally, so their suppliers should not be excluded from demonopolisation on the basis that foreign competition will be effective.

2.2 Markets with easy entry

For markets into which entry is relatively free, demonopolisation may not significantly increase the level of competition. In such markets, the new competition provided by entry can constrain anti-competitive behav-iour by incumbent producers in two ways: enterprises may enter the market and reduce the dominance of even a former monopolist; and enterprises may credibly threaten to enter in the event of anti-competitive behaviour. Regardless of which mechanism is the more important, demonopolisation would not further directly change the com-petitiveness of markets characterised by easy entry.

Incumbent concentration may affect indirectly the ability of entry to constrain anti-competitive behaviour. A monopolist (or concentrated industry) may be able to threaten credibly a lower post-entry price than unconcentrated incumbents can threaten, thereby more strongly deter-ring entry. In Eastern Europe, however, old monopolists will likely use older, less efficient technologies than new entrants would use. In demon-opolising economies under such circumstances, the threat of a low post-entry price is not credible (except when incumbents are state-subsidised). Hence, this indirect effect is less likely to be a problem in fully privatised markets.

For entry to ensure long-term competitive behaviour in a market with a concentrated structure, three conditions must hold: entry into the market must be timely, of sufficiently large scale, and likely in the event of anti-competitive behaviour in the market. The Canadian competition agency, for example, directs its 'assessment . . . toward determining whether entry by potential competitors would likely occur on a sufficient scale in response to a material price increase . . . to ensure that such a price increase could not be sustained for more than two years.' Markets are less likely to satisfy these conditions for easy entry in economies undergoing radical transformations than in established economies. Even if the particular good has characteristics that make entry into its production or sale sufficiently easy, an 'economic infrastructure' must be in place; there must be unhindered markets for inputs, including capital and an effective legal infrastructure. If these conditions do not hold, as they do not in many transforming economies, then entry may not limit anti-competitive behaviour and demonopolisation may be advisable.

One factor that may offset the difficulties inherent in market entry in a transitional economy is technological change. Relative production costs enter importantly into an enterprise's decision to enter a market. If everything else is equal, entry is more likely when the entrants would use production methods with lower costs than the incumbents' methods, than when the two types of enterprises would have the same production costs. Thus, if existing monopolies have obsolete, high-cost production technologies and new competitors in transforming economies can readily import lower-cost production technologies from abroad, then entry may be easy and demonopolisation may be unnecessary.

In markets for which entry is sufficiently difficult that the decision is made to demonopolise the current supplier, entry conditions might nevertheless influence the partition decision. The demonopolisation partition would be less critical if subsequent large changes in market structure were expected. Such changes might result from substantial entry by new or foreign enterprises, or from technological change that quickly renders the present physical assets obsolete.

2.3 Alternatives to demonopolisation

Some industries have such large economies of extent over the extent of the relevant market that only one or a few enterprises can efficiently supply the market. Smaller producers would have such a large cost penalty that they would be uneconomic. Such industries may include the local distribution of electricity, natural gas and some areas of telecommunications. If multiple producers cannot efficiently produce because of these economies, then some means of limiting inefficient or anti-competitive behaviour other than demonopolisation must be sought. Four options are outlined here.

One solution may be to privatise and regulate the monopoly. In some cases, part of a state enterprise might be demonopolised to compete in markets and part might remain a regulated monopoly. In such cases, absent effective safeguards, complete separation might be preferable to continued integration in order to prevent, for example, subsidisation of the competitive part by the regulated part. Government agencies regulate, directly or indirectly, the prices charged by these enterprises and can influence their investment decisions.

A second possible solution for the control of monopolies that cannot be demonopolised is state ownership and management. It is widely believed, however, that generally state-owned enterprises are not managed efficiently.

A third alternative is to privatise the monopoly, accept monopoly pricing in the short term, and reduce barriers to competition from other products or enterprises. The advantage of an unregulated, private monopoly over a state-owned monopoly is that the private monopoly would have incentives to be internally efficient whereas the state-owned monopoly would not.

A fourth possible solution is for the state to retain ownership of the monopoly's assets but to auction to private enterprises the right to operate the monopoly, and retain its profits, for a fixed period of time. If the periods are sufficiently long, then the private 'temporary owner' will make efficient technology choices. If the rights of 'temporary ownership' are sold at a competitive auction, the state's revenue will be equal to the value of the monopoly profits. Therefore, the monopoly profits go to the state rather than to the private owner of a permanent monopoly. But monopoly pricing remains, with its attendant inefficiencies.

2.4 Conclusion

This section has identified characteristics of markets that need not be demonopolised: markets in which low transportation costs and low import barriers permit effective foreign competition; markets with sufficiently easy entry that actual or potential entrants limit anticompetitive behaviour by monopolistic incumbents; and markets with large-scale economies for which alternatives to demonopolisation may produce better results. However, many industries will not fall into these categories. State-owned enterprises in those industries should be broken apart in the privatisation process.

3. Partitioning monopoly enterprises

Having decided to demonopolise a particular enterprise, the next task is to determine how to partition it. This section considers ways to break apart monopolistic state enterprises so that the resulting daughter enterprises are efficiently configured. The next section will consider how to evaluate competition in the markets they supply.

In any enterprise, a variety of assets work together to transform the enterprise's inputs into intermediate and final outputs. Rational demonopolisation requires an understanding of the relationships among the assets within the enterprise. Some sets of assets might require common ownership for efficient operation; separating them into different enterprises would result in higher production costs. Other sets of assets might supply competing products: assigning them to the same enterprises would reduce competition. This section is, therefore, primarily a discussion of relationships among assets.

The two major types of relationships are horizontal and vertical. Two assets are related vertically if the output of one (the 'upstream' asset) is the input of the other (the 'downstream' asset). Two assets are related horizontally if they supply the same relevant market. For example, a production plant and its distribution network are vertically related, but two production plants that make the same product in the same town are horizontally related. The first subsection focuses on reasons for assets to be commonly owned, with most attention on vertical relationships. The subsequent sections focus on horizontal relationships among assets.

In practice, demonopolisation choices are constrained by sunk investments. For example, if machines are grouped together in a single factory, then assigning them to separate enterprises would require either that some of the machines be moved or that there be continuing negotiation by the separate enterprises over necessarily common inputs such as real estate and utilities. If these additional costs are large, then the machines must be assigned to the same enterprise by the demonopolising authority.

3.1 Benefits of integration

Market transactions, contracts and integration are alternative ways in which assets can be related to one another. When failures of contracts or market transactions among assets would result in sufficiently large inefficiencies, then those assets should be assigned by the demonopolising authority to the same enterprise. This subsection identifies some cases in which the efficiency losses from non-integration are likely to be large.

Enterprises may use contracts to specify the characteristics of the products they buy and sell. However, sometimes it is too expensive, or impossible, to describe all the relevant characteristics in such a way that an independent arbiter, such as a court, could determine whether the terms of the contract were met. In particular, the contract might not adequately describe all the relevant characteristics of the product, its delivery schedule, the terms of the contract under all possible circumstances and so on. The contract might also be one for which a court cannot observe whether the terms of the contract are met. At other times, the terms of a contract cannot be specified under changing conditions, such as periods of unanticipated demand or after unanticipated technological change.

If a country's contract law is not well developed, then contracts may be more expensive to enforce, or enforcement may be more uncertain, than in countries where contract law is better developed. Therefore, in such countries, it may be more efficient to have more assets held within single enterprises than would otherwise be the case. In some sense, of course, 'ownership' is just the substitution of one form of contract for another. In other words, common ownership is a solution to an incomplete contracting problem to the extent that 'ownership' imparts certain other rights that 'fill in the gaps' of the incomplete contract. Such ownership rights may, however, generate different types of inefficiencies. For example, hired managers and workers may need to be monitored to ensure optimal behaviour.

Two benefits of integration that should be considered in making demonopolisation decisions are the avoidance of 'hold up' problems, and the facilitation of the co-ordination of assets when the costs of faulty co-ordination are high.

'Hold up' occurs when one enterprise must make idiosyncratic investments to use the output from another enterprise and no adequate contract can be written. For example, a coal mine may build a rail spur to a specific railroad. After the mine builds the spur, changing to a different supplier of rail transportation would be costly. The mine faces a monopolist; its next best alternative may be building another expensive rail spur to another railroad. The price offered by the monopolistic railroad will not be the competitive price, so the mine buys a smaller than optimum quantity of rail transportation. If the two enterprises were owned and managed together to maximise profits, then one enterprise would not 'hold up' the other, and the optimal quantity of the good (rail transportation, in this example) would be traded between them. Therefore, when demonopolising, assets that could substantially 'hold up' other assets should be placed together into the same enterprise.

Co-ordination of assets may be easier if they are held in the same enterprise, under common ownership and management, than if they are held in separate enterprises. The efficiencies arising from vertical integration are apparent in a comparison of the following examples. One example is of a relationship that is commonly contractual, without integration, while the other relationship is usually one of common ownership. A compressor is a pre-assembled component in a room air conditioner. The compressors must have specific physical characteristics and must be delivered to the air conditioner manufacturer according to a schedule. Co-ordination between the compressor factory and the air conditioner factory is achievable through a contract, enforceable through the courts, because the design of the air conditioners does not change very often or unpredictably: it is possible to specify each of the physical characteristics required of the compressor and the delivery schedule in a way that the parties to the contract are satisfied and a court can determine whether the terms of a supply contract are met. Integration is not required. Hence, an integrated compressor plus air conditioner manufacturing enterprise could be dissolved, without loss of efficiencies, by the demonopolising authority.

The second example of a vertical relationship highlights the advantages of common ownership. This example involves a blast furnace and a primary reduction mill in steel production. In steel production, the metal must be delivered from the blast furnace in a molten state, at the correct time, at the correct temperature, and with a chemical composition within certain specifications. It may be impossible to write an enforceable, comprehensive contract for this vertical relationship because the demands of the downstream processes change frequently and unpredicta-bly, so that they would be difficult to specify beforehand. Effective, enforceable standards describing the quality of output provided by the blast furnace may also be difficult to specify in a way that can be verified later by an independent arbiter (such as a court). Such stages of pro-duction should not be separated during demonopolisation.

Where there are no large cost savings from integration, vertically integrated enterprises compete in markets with non-integrated enter-prises. For example, some room air conditioner manufacturers produce their own compressors while others buy compressors from other enter-prises. Another example is provided by corrugators and carton-making machines. A corrugator is a machine that produces corrugated board from paper and glue. Carton-making machines are an array of machines that cut, print and fold the corrugated board to transform it into corru-gated board cartons. Often in the United States, the corrugator and the downstream carton-making machines are owned by the same enterprise and located in the same building. Sometimes, however, the corrugator and carton-making machines are owned by separate enterprises and located several miles apart. In this industry, operations that are related by market transactions and by integrated ownership exist simul-taneously, although each type of enterprise tends to specialise in the production of distinct types of cartons. When enterprises with different degrees of integration suffer little or no cost penalties, the daughter enterprises that result from demonopolisation need not have the same degree of vertical integration.

3.2 *Assets that supply the same relevant market*

Demonopolisation decisions regarding the ownership of assets that supply the same relevant market are critical because the structure of the ownership of such assets affects the competitive conduct of private enter-prises in that market. The primary way in which demonopolisation can ensure competition is in separating those assets into different enter-prises, creating multiple competitors.

There is no minimum number of competitors necessary for 'sufficient' competition in a given market. Economic theory does not give a definitive number, and while many empirical economics papers have attempted to determine the relationship between the number and size of suppliers and the degree of competition in markets, they have not been fully successful. But a rough idea of a sufficient number of competitors can be inferred from the merger guidelines published by various competition agencies. These guidelines, which employ structural measures of markets as starting-points for analysis, can guide observers on whether a proposed merger is likely to create or enhance 'market power'. 'Market power' is defined as the 'ability of one or more firms profitably to maintain prices above competitive levels for a significant period of time.' The application for which these guidelines are designed, the evaluation of the competitive effect of the loss of one independent enterprise, is potentially a less complex problem than that of demonopolisation. Demonopolisation requires the evaluation of a greater number and variety of possible market structures while, simultaneously, upstream and downstream markets are changing radically. However, the merger guidelines use measurable, structural characteristics, along with other observable factors, to evaluate the level of competition in those markets. Although imperfect, these guides are the only ones available that have been developed by investigators who have evaluated competition in numerous and various markets.

The structural concentration measures in the guidelines of the US Department of Justice imply that, for example, absent further information about a market, a change from six to five equally sized competitors would be considered likely substantially to lessen competition, except in extraordinary cases. In particular, the guidelines state that, if a merger increases the Herfindahl-Hirschman Index ('HHI', the sum of squares of enterprises' market shares, expressed in percentages) by more than 100, resulting in a post-merger HHI substantially exceeding 1,800, then 'only in extraordinary cases will [other] factors establish that the merger is not likely substantially to lessen competition'. A change from six equally sized competitors to five equally sized competitors changes the HHI from 1,667 to 2,000. The Canadian Bureau of Competition Policy, if it had no further information about a market, would consider a market with several equally sized competitors to be unlikely to behave anti-competitively. Specifically, according to the guidelines, a merger leaving the market with a four-firm concentration ratio (the percentage of the market held by the four largest enterprises) below 65 per cent is considered 'unlikely to have anti-competitive consequences'. A market with seven equal-size competitors has a four-firm concentration ratio of four-sevenths, or 57 per cent.

In practice, more information than the number of competitors would be available, both for merger evaluation and demonopolisation. For example, as discussed above, entry by new domestic enterprises or by foreign suppliers can diminish or eliminate anti-competitive behaviour in markets. Nevertheless, these structural measures can be used as a starting-point to indicate the approximate degree of demonopolisation – the approximate number of separate enterprises – that is more likely to result in competitive market behaviour.

The demonopolisation of assets with significant economies of scale up to a relatively large scale presents special problems. 'Excess' demonopolisation of assets that exhibit economies of scale may create daughter enterprises that are too small to exploit these economies. As a result, their production costs would be unnecessarily high. Alternatively, there are advantages to having more competitors: the price of the good is likely to be closer to the cost of production. But when scale economies are large, such advantages must be weighed against the advantages of fewer enterprises: the reduction of production costs. In practice, the crucial question is whether the magnitude of the cost increase resulting from splitting assets among an additional enterprise is sufficiently large that those cost increases outweigh the price decrease.

A decision to preserve scale economies of enterprises in one relevant market may, if there are strong incentives to vertically integrate, preclude some demonopolisation choices in upstream or downstream markets. Economic theory has little definitive to say about the welfare effects of vertical integration of oligopolistic markets. The issue depends upon the minimum efficient scale (the smallest level of output at which minimum cost is achieved) of the activities in question. Empirical observation suggests that even when the minimum efficient scale of one activity is large relative to those of other activities undertaken by an enterprise, the returns to vertical integration are sometimes large enough to justify integration even if some activities are undertaken on an inefficiently small scale. Further, as enterprises integrate, independent suppliers become fewer, which induces more buyers to vertically integrate. In the extreme, this can result in the disappearance of markets for the intermediate product. In making demonopolisation decisions, therefore, the efficiencies of vertical integration and operation at large scale must be weighed against the loss of competition in intermediate markets, and perhaps the loss of the intermediate market itself. If a market disappears, then entry into either the upstream or downstream market would require simultaneous entry into both levels. This effect can raise entry costs, further reducing competition. However, such a disappearance of an intermediate market is likely to present a problem only in those cases where the intermediate product cannot be imported.

3.3 Intellectual property

In dividing horizontally related assets, attention must be paid to the division of a state enterprise's intellectual property among the daughter enterprises. If patents, licenses, blueprints and information accumulated through experience are improperly divided, then enterprises could be left without legal access to the technology they use and without the means of servicing old equipment or installed products. This problem could be avoided if intellectual property were distributed so that each daughter enterprise had the intellectual property (including patents, licenses and blueprints) that it applies to its physical assets. In order to facilitate competition in the servicing of installed products, the intellectual property associated with those sales (e.g. equipment installation and repair records) might be made available on a non-discriminatory basis to all daughter enterprises. However, in many countries, such a wholesale redistribution of intellectual property would violate the principles established by patent systems that give innovators property rights to their inventions.

Conclusion

In this section, the ways in which assets can be related and the implications of those relationships for demonopolisation were discussed. Each application of these principles will be different, with different trade-offs. The resulting enterprises may be of quite different configurations, of varying size and varying degrees of vertical integration. These variations might be present within the same market because the sunk investments – the physical assets as they are found – constrain the demonopolisation decisions.

Once the boundaries of the daughter enterprises are provisionally delineated, the degree of competition in markets in which they will compete must be evaluated. This is the topic of the next section.

4. Evaluation of competition

To this point, demonopolisation has been examined from within a fissuring state enterprise. Another perspective is that of markets: if the proposed demonopolisation is unlikely to induce competition in markets, then the demonopolisation plan must be re-examined or other changes must be made.

One starting-point in evaluating the likely competitiveness of a market is its structure. In demonopolising industries with no experience with free markets, sales cannot be measured, but capacities – or at least, quantities that could be supplied at marginal cost lower than some specified level – might be measurable. Once a metric for measuring enterprise size has been chosen, the level of concentration in the market can be calculated. Note, though, that assets that will exit their current market should be assigned zero weight. For example, some assets of state monopolists may not be profitable in competitive markets because they apply outdated, inefficient technology. If these assets could not be made profitable with an investment of capital embodying new technology, then it seems reasonable to assume that these assets will not operate after privatisation. They must either exit their market or continue to operate and be subsidised by the state. If the assets leave their current market, then the weight they are assigned for evaluating competition should be zero.

Various competition authorities use a variety of concentration measures to characterise the degree of competition in a market. For example, the US Department of Justice measures concentration by the sum of squares of all the individual enterprises' market shares. If this sum exceeds 1,800, then it considers that market to be 'highly concentrated'. For a market of five equally sized competitors, this sum would equal 2,000. The Canadian Bureau of Competition Policy measures concentration by the sum of the four largest enterprises' market shares. If this sum exceeds 65 per cent, then the market is considered to have increased potential for anti-competitive behaviour. In a market with seven equally sized competitors this sum would equal 57 per cent. The European Communities competition authority measures a single enterprise's market share. As that share becomes larger, it is increasingly likely for the competition authority to consider it to be dominant, i.e. to be freer to act without regard to competitors' actions.

If by the above measures, a market appears to have a 'concentrated' structure, further investigation of the market is required. The Canadian competition authority, for example, considers several additional factors: likely future entry, likely sources of 'domestic or foreign potential competition', 'barriers to expansion that would likely be faced by [enterprises] within the market', types of rivalry within the market (e.g. 'aggressive pricing strategies, innovative distribution . . . methods, product . . . innovation and aggressive service offerings') and the competitive nature of particular enterprises. Information about entry barriers, potential competitors and capacity expansion may be available prior to the free operation of the market. As discussed above, entry into a market can constrain anti-competitive behaviour. Similarly, expansion by enterprises that already supply the market can constrain anti-competitive behaviour by the other suppliers. If these responses to anti-competitive behaviour would be adequate, then generally even a concentrated market would behave competitively.

In the above evaluation of market structure, the supplying enterprises were assumed to be privately owned. However, state-owned or subsidised enterprises may persist for some time in the transforming economies. The nature of competition in markets where private and state-subsidised enterprises compete is not well understood. The incentives and constraints on the managers of state-subsidised enterprises are likely to differ from those of privately owned enterprises. While it is likely that state-subsidised enterprises distort competition, the direction of the effect is not known.

The above discussion is intended to be only a brief overview of how competition might be assessed in order to provide a 'feedback loop' for demonopolisation partitions. If the structure of a market under a proposed partition appears to be too concentrated and other characteristics of the market make anti-competitive behaviour more likely, then a re-examination of the demonopolisation partition, reduction of market entry barriers, reduction of imports barriers, or alternatives to demonopolisation must be considered.

5. Demonopolising example

This section provides an example of the demonopolisation of a vertically integrated food retailer. Although simplified, this example illustrates the examination of horizontal and vertical relationships between assets and the effect of economies of scale at one level on the ownership structure of another level. The example is a hypothetical one; in practice, entry barriers into food retailing are likely to be sufficiently low that careful demonopolisation would be unnecessary.

Assume that a single enterprise, named 'StateFoods', owns all the retail food stores and a small fraction of the warehouses in a city. For simplicity, assume that a retail food store sells only shelf-stable food (e.g. canned foods, flour, sugar, rice and pasta), which does not require special handling. The warehouses are used to store food before they are distributed to the retail stores. StateFoods obtains the food through supply contracts with food processors and food importers.

The analysis begins with identifying the relevant markets that the assets held by StateFoods will supply after the economic transformation. Making a few additional assumptions and applying the approximate method in the Appendix, the relevant product markets may be found to be warehousing and food retailing. If sufficiently expensive modifications of warehouses were necessary for them to be used for food storage, then one relevant product market would be food warehousing rather than all warehousing. It is likely that food store customers will not travel far to buy food since the trip must be made frequently. Therefore, the geographic markets over which retail food stores compete are relatively small, perhaps a few kilometres in radius or less. Because the cost of transporting a truck over a few kilometres is small relative to the value of a truckload of food, a geographic market for warehouses is likely to be a city or large portion thereof.

The second step is to a determination whether to demonopolise, applying the concepts of Section 2. Foreign competition is unlikely. If the input markets (for example, the wholesale food markets and real estate market) worked well, effective competition from new entrants is likely: under such circumstances, a single retail store would not suffer significant cost disadvantages relative to the incumbent and the sunk capital costs would be relatively small. In such circumstances, demonopolisation would be unnecessary. For the sake of the example, though, the decision to demonopolise is assumed.

Next, the relationships among the assets owned by StateFoods are considered, applying the concepts discussed above in Section 3. Retail stores use warehouses to hold their inventory since there is insufficient storage space in the stores. Therefore, the stores require timely delivery from the warehouses. If a store often has an insufficient inventory, then customers would quit buying food from it – they would go instead to a store that usually has food available – and the store would eventually exit the market.

The necessary co-ordination between stores and warehouses might be achieved in a number of ways. The same enterprises could own both the stores and the warehouses. Alternatively, separate enterprises could own the warehouses, lease them to the stores, and the stores manage the warehouses. A third alternative is for separate enterprises to both own and manage the warehouses, so that the stores simply buy food from the warehouse owner, who is now a wholesale food broker. The choice among these three (and more) alternatives is based upon at least the following considerations: the state of contract law, and economies of scale in the provision of food warehousing.

If contract law is not well developed, so that a store cannot be confident that terms of contracts will be met, then the store may need to own and operate its own warehouse. Because (by assumption) StateFoods owns only a small fraction of the warehouses in the city, such a solution would not be likely to affect significantly the level of competition in the warehouse market. Alternatively, if contract law is poorly developed but there are many food brokers in the city, the store might simply buy from the food broker. The credible threat of lost customers may limit the extent to which brokers do not fulfil their contracts.

If there are significant economies of scale in the provision of food warehousing, so that the per-store cost of food warehousing is substantially lower when a warehouse serves several retail stores than when it serves one, then there are two likely efficient configurations: retail stores remain independent and buy from food brokers, or retail stores are grouped into chains. In the first configuration, food brokers may be sufficiently large that they can fully exploit the economies of scale and there may be enough competition among brokers that those cost savings are passed onto the retail stores. In the second configuration, each enterprise owns one or more warehouses and enough retail stores to exhaust the economies of scale at the warehousing level. If the state of contract law is such that stores and warehouses must be owned by the same enterprise, and food brokers do not provide an adequate alternative, then the second configuration would be superior.

Finally, the level of competition in the relevant markets, under the provisional demonopolisation plan, is evaluated, using the procedure of Section 4. In this example, this evaluation is relatively simple. By assumption, the warehousing market is very unconcentrated, so it is likely to be competitive. The retail food store markets are likely to be competitive if each few square kilometres' area has a number of retail stores. If the stores were grouped into chains, then losses of competition among retail stores can be minimised by having each small area served by several different chains.

6. Conclusions

Demonopolisation is but one component in the transformation of the formerly centrally planned economies of Eastern Europe into market economies. Demonopolisation is a critical step in creating competition in such economies. Therefore, competition officials should be involved in making demonopolisation decisions. Each part of the micro-economic transformation is linked with the others so that, for example, demonopolisation decisions may be affected by the robustness of capital and real estate markets, the level of import tariffs and the convertibility of the currency. Therefore, there can be no single 'demonopolisation method' policy prescription. In many countries, demonopolisation may be undertaken with inadequate information and insufficient time to evaluate the available information. In such an environment, the 'rules of thumb' developed from basic industrial organisation economics described above may be the most appropriate guides.

7. Appendix

7.1 Relevant markets: definition and a method for approximate delineation in the absence of price information

Successful demonopolisation requires some knowledge of relevant markets, the arenas in which competition among enterprises occurs. Without this knowledge, assets that could compete to supply the same relevant market (i.e. be assigned to separate enterprises in demonopolisation) might be incorrectly assigned to the same enterprise, resulting in diminished competition in that market. Alternatively, assets that supply distinct markets might be unnecessarily assigned to separate enterprises, possibly resulting in higher production costs. Ideally, therefore, relevant markets should be defined before state enterprises are demonopolised.

This strategy cannot be adopted, however, because relevant markets are endogenously determined in the demonopolisation process. Relevant markets cannot be delineated without knowing, or accurately estimating, prices. Prices are the outcomes of political processes (that set, for example, import tariffs, tax rates, subsidies and regulations). Prices are also the outcomes of decisions about ownership demonopolisation itself. If a method for delineating markets that does not use prices can be found, then a strategy of first delineating markets, then applying that knowledge to breaking apart state enterprises, can be followed. Such an approach would avoid the endogeneity problem, but it would not always accurately delineate relevant markets. This Appendix suggests a simple methodology for approximate delineation of relevant markets in the absence of prices that can be used for making demonopolisation decisions.

7.2 Market definition with known prices

A relevant market has two important dimensions, product and geographic. It is defined so that products within a relevant market are relatively close substitutes for one another, but that products excluded from the relevant market are not close substitutes for products in the relevant market. If there is a continuum of products, however, then products just outside the relevant market would be close substitutes for products just inside the market. One formal definition of relevant market is that it is a 'product or group of products and a geographic area in which it is sold such that a hypothetical, profit-maximising firm, not subject to price regulation, that was the only present and future seller of those products in that area would impose a "small but significant and nontransitory" increase in price above prevailing or likely future levels'. A relevant market must contain products that are close substitutes with other products in the relevant market. If it did not, then many buyers would respond to the hypothetical price increase by switching to the substitute product, decreasing sales of the product that is in the candidate relevant market, and the hypothetical monopolist's price increase would not be profit-maximising. A relevant market generally contains only products that are close substitutes, because in general, the smallest group of products meeting the definition is taken to be the relevant market.

The definition of a relevant market relies upon the prices, or likely future prices, of all the products that might be substitutes. In particular, the buyers of a product at a given price will consider the prices of that product's possible substitutes in deciding whether, in response to a hypothetical price increase, to switch to buying one of the possible substitutes or to continue buying the original product. If the prices that are used in defining relevant markets are unknown and incorrectly predicted, then buyers' substitution choices may be incorrectly predicted. If this results in incorrectly drawing the boundary of the relevant market, the suppliers to the relevant market may be incorrectly identified and therefore the level of competition within the relevant market may be incorrectly predicted.

For example, if diesel fuel were currently subsidised and the current price of diesel were used to determine the distance over which gravel can be economically transported, then falsely 'large' geographic markets for gravel could be delineated. If, after the economic transition is completed, the price of diesel rose to the world price, then the true distance over which gravel may be transported economically would become apparent, and it may become apparent that distant gravel pits do not compete with each other. If, in demonopolising, it had been assumed that distant gravel pits competed, then nearby gravel pits may have been assigned to the same enterprise. In this case, the degree of actual competition that results from the faulty 'demonopolisation' is less than would have resulted had the correct price of diesel fuel been used to delineate geographic markets and make demonopolisation decisions.

7.3 The difficulty of predicting prices before demonopolisation

In general, it is impossible to predict accurately the prices that will prevail after the economic transformation of an economy: market prices are hard to predict outcomes of complex interactions among market actors and of political forces. Prices set by central planners or distorted by monopolies are, in general, different from those that would prevail after an economy is privatised, demonopolised and otherwise transformed. The outcomes of political decisions affect prices: some products may be subsidised; some products may be taxed more heavily than others; regulations that affect the cost of some activity may be imposed; and some industries may be protected by import barriers from foreign competition.

Further, given taxes, subsidies and regulations, the cost functions and strategies of suppliers in a market vary with differences in the ownership structure of productive assets. For example, consider the machines or factories that can produce a given good. A monopoly owner would have a different cost function and face a different apparent demand function, and therefore probably would have a different pricing or production strategy, from those of several owners of the same assets. Hence, the equilibrium price of that good would be different, if the assets were owned by a monopolist, from what it would have been had those assets been owned by several distinct owners. In this way, demonopolisation decisions affect prices and, through them, the boundaries of relevant markets. Accordingly, relevant markets are endogenously determined in demonopolisation.

The major exception to the conclusion that prices can be affected by changes in the structure of domestic industry are markets with substantial international trade or with particularly free entry. In markets with substantial international trade, the domestic price may be the price that results from the interaction of buyers and sellers throughout the world. If this is so, then the domestic industry structure and any changes that might result from its demonopolisation will not affect the domestic price.

7.4 Method of delineating relevant markets when prices are unknown

Because the means of delineating relevant markets using prices cannot easily be applied directly to an economy undergoing radical change, an approximation of relevant markets must be employed. We present here a method of approximation. Under this method, if three conditions are met, then products are considered to be in the same relevant market. If the three conditions are not met, then products are considered to be in separate relevant markets. Although this method is not the best way in principle to delineate a relevant market, it has the advantages of being applicable to an economy with no meaningful prices and, under certain conditions, or correctly delineating relevant markets. By this rule, the two conditions that, together, are sufficient and necessary for products to be in the same relevant product market are (1) they are physically similar and (2) their production costs are likely, after the transition, to be similar. The geographic market considerations, which provides the third condition for products to be in the same relevant market, are addressed later.

The choice of delineation method was affected by the use to which the approximate relevant markets would be put. The markets will be used to make decisions about breaking apart monopolistic state enterprises. With sufficient care to preserve large enterprises when there are large economies of scale and sufficiently careful subsequent merger policy, it seems likely that the potential loss from insufficient demonopolisation is greater than the potential loss from too much demonopolisation. Therefore, this method is more likely to make the error of not recognising a competitor – of not recognising that a product actually competes in the same relevant market as another – than to make the error of incorrectly identifying a non-competing product as being in the relevant market.

The main error that results from using this rule is a failure to recognise that two products may be substitutes when one product is low quality and low priced but its substitute is high quality and high priced. Two products may be in the same relevant market, i.e. be close substitutes, but have significantly different physical characteristics and prices. They are close substitutes because buyers consider the higher-priced product to have some attribute – for example, higher energy efficiency or greater reliability – so that the costs to the buyers of using them are approximately the same. In such case, small changes in relative price cause buyers to substitute between the higher-priced and the lower-priced product. The rule for defining relevant markets used in this paper would not identify substitutes of this type. The definition of substitute used in this paper is an approximation, designed to be practicably usable where there are no meaningful prices. The error of not identifying substitutes of the type described here is difficult if not impossible to avoid when prices are unpredictable.

The first condition that the products are physically similar, is designed to make it more likely that buyers would consider them to be physical substitutes in the use for which they are purchased. If the goods are not sufficiently physically similar, then the substitution of one good for another may require buyers to make additional capital expenditures or to change the other inputs. If switching costs were large, then buyers would not make the investment and would not consider the other product to be a substitute. In practice, determining the limits of a relevant market often requires considering more than just the physical characteristics of a product. Reliability of supply, reliability of quality, uniformity of physical characteristics, speed and quality of technical service, spare parts availability, breadth of product offering, financial health of the supplier and other characteristics may be important to buyers. In such cases, enterprises that make apparently physically similar products in fact do not sell products that buyers consider to be substitutes.

The second condition, that post-transition production costs of the goods are likely to be approximately the same, is designed to ensure that the prices of the goods will be similar. If goods are identical, are produced in the same location, and have identical production costs, then, subject to certain technical assumptions about information and transaction costs, their prices will be identical in a market equilibrium. The explanation is, in essence, that if the products are physically identified, offered at the same location, and buyers costlessly know all this, then buyers' actions would force suppliers to offer the identical price. If enterprises have identical production costs, then they can each offer the same price.

For goods to be in the same relevant market, they must be produced in the same geographic market. Determining, in the absence of prices, whether two producers are located in the same geographic market can be difficult because transportation costs are commonly the most important factor in determining the size of geographic markets. Other factors that limit shipments of a product might be fragility or perishability, or the need to provide services which cannot be provided at long distances. Some products are commonly traded over large distances in well-developed market economies. For these products, only very large differences between the cost of transportation in a market economy and in a transforming economy would sufficiently change the size of geographic markets to the extent that demonopolisation decisions would be affected. In these cases, it may be reasonable to assume that the size of geographic markets in the emerging economy will not differ substantially from those of the established market economies.

However, for products with relatively small geographic markets, e.g. city-sized markets, demonopolisation decisions could be affected by significant differences in geographic markets. If transportation costs will be about the same in the transforming economy as in the well-developed market economies, then the sizes of geographic markets for the same products in the market economies might provide a good approximation for the sizes of geographic markets in the transforming economy. If transportation costs will differ significantly from those in established market economies, then further investigation might reveal that factors other than transportation costs are significant determinants of geographic markets. For example, it may be learned that ease of information exchange between supplier and buyer is very important, and short distances are necessary for this information exchange. In this case, it might be found that geographic markets are likely to be small, even though transportation costs may be unknown. If this method were to be inapplicable, but estimates of transportation costs and product prices could be made, then another approximation method might be used. By this method, the maximum ratio of transportation costs to product price for a specific product is found for a market economy. Then, the distance in the transforming economy at which the ratio of transportation cost to product price is the same is calculated. This distance is used as the radius of geographic markets for that product. This method of geographic market delineation, however, is not very accurate and requires price estimates. Hence, it must be used with care.

CONCLUSIONS

Saul Estrin and Martin Cave

1. Competition Policy in Transition

This volume contains contributions from practitioners of competition policy in the economies in transition, as well as their counterparts in Western Europe and the United States and academic experts. The intention has been to highlight similarities and contrasts in legal arrangements and evolving practice between Western countries and the previously planned economies, as well as differences within the latter group. Though our attention has focused on the countries most advanced in the transformation process – the Czech and Slovak Federal Republic, Hungary and Poland – the issues are common to the region, and there should be much in these pages for legislators and practitioners in the Balkans and the former Soviet Union.

Our aim in this chapter is to draw together the strands that have been running through the book, and to offer some final thoughts about the appropriate model for competition policy in transition. We start by posing the counterfactual; could the transition process be proceeding equally satisfactorily without any competition policy? We argue strongly in the following section that such a policy is required, and go on to highlight in Section 3 the special characteristics of actual competition policy in the countries under consideration, including the role of the EC Articles of Association. We conclude by reflecting more generally on the role of the state in economic transformation, arguing that it is a misjudgement to rely excessively on the 'invisible hand' to achieve transition to a competitive market economy in a situation when entrepreneurial skills are rusty or underdeveloped and the market structure is severely imperfect.

2. Is competition policy necessary?

The role of competition policy, in developed market economies at least, is reasonably well understood. It is ultimately to protect consumers from the negative welfare consequences of excessive product market monopoly power. It affects three general areas: market structure, business conduct and company performance. Competition policy relating to structure aims principally to thwart the development of unacceptably monopolised markets, for example through mergers. Legislation on conduct is concerned to prevent firms from acting to exploit market imperfections and performance can be controlled directly, for example through price controls.

It has been argued that legislation on competition policy is completely unnecessary, if not actually welfare-reducing, because free markets will themselves ensure sufficient competitiveness to guarantee consumer welfare without public intervention. One line has been to hypothesise that, while firms are undoubtably larger and markets less competitive than the model of perfect competition requires, this may not have a serious effect on welfare. Theory suggests that, even if there are only a limited number of firms in a market, outcomes may still approximate those under competition provided that they do not collude in setting output or price. For example, if numerous firms compete over market shares according to the Cournot model, prices and therefore welfare, approximate the competitive levels. Moreover, according to the Bertrand model, if firms compete over price and provided goods are homogeneous, markets will achieve the competitive price-quantity combination, even if there are only two firms. Observed, rather imperfect, market structures combined with competitive behaviour may therefore be enough to deliver high consumer welfare without policy intervention. It has also been argued (following Harberger, 1954) that monopoly welfare losses in practice are not very large in Western economies.

The second argument refers to the growing importance of international trade in domestic consumption. If an economy is open to international competition, little can be deduced about the degree of competition in consumer markets by studying the number and size distribution of domestic suppliers. Foreign firms can provide the competition to prevent domestic firms from abusing domestic market imperfections. The argument that international trade can substitute for competition policy seems particularly strong for products of the manufacturing sector, which are more easily traded, and for countries where tariffs are low and exchange rates are convertible. It is less persuasive for partially or non-traded goods, including many services; in larger economies for which trade is relatively less significant; and when exchange rates are undervalued so the prices of imported goods are high.

Whether or not one has sympathy with this proposition for Western economies, the contributions in this book suggest that it is much less convincing for the economies in transition. As we have seen, market structures were severely imperfect at the time when prices were liberalised, far more so than in comparable Western countries, and the mentality of planning had ingrained in management the habit of collusion. In consequence, it has proved very hard to establish competitive practices in the existing state-owned sector. For example, monopoly power is widely seen as an important contributing factor in the failure of relative prices to adjust to demand following 'big bang' stabilisation programmes. Newbery and Kattuman (1992) have further argued that because the imperfect market structures reduce incentives for efficiency, they are a major cause of the soft budget constraint and thus a major explanatory factor in the continuing poor economic performance of state-owned firms.

A seeming counterargument concerns the potential impact of trade. The countries upon which we have focused all have high shares of trade in final output, have dramatically liberalised their trade regimes and have introduced currency convertibility. Foreign competition could in principle substitute for domestic competitive market pressures, and therefore reduce the required scope of policy intervention. However, there are a number of qualifications, the most significant of which concerns the exchange rate. Many of the economies in transition introduced convertibility with severely undervalued exchange rates. The consequence was that in the early phases of transition, foreign competition in practice played only a limited role in countering monopolistic abuses. Particularly in Poland, rising domestic prices later eradicated the under valuation and brought foreign firms' prices in line with those of internal suppliers. However, as noted in the Polish contribution, the resulting deterioration in the balance of payments quickly brought pressures for an increase in tariffs and other trade restrictions. Trade must also be less significant for competition in large economies, such as that of Russia.

The problem with relying on international competition rather than domestic policy to counter abuse of monopoly power is that it is probably neither feasible nor credible. The countries in question have limited foreign exchange reserves, and are likely to face very high levels of unemployment in the medium term as they restructure away from heavy and defence industries. Moreover, domestic suppliers are for the most part financially weak, inexperienced in operating in a market system and competitive in neither price nor quality. In order to rely on international competition the authorities must be able to finance the balance of payments deficits which will result. They must also accept the higher unemployment resulting from the bankrupting of firms which have not learnt quickly enough that the government is willing to use imports to substitute for excessively priced domestic goods. As the Polish case makes clear, it seems unlikely that governments in transition, after the first flush of the 'big bang', will consistently stick with such draconian solutions to the problems of domestic market power. We see evidence for this conclusion in all our contributions; anti-monopoly offices everywhere are particularly sensitive to the charge of further undermining the debilitated state of domestic suppliers.

We can conclude that the standard arguments for competition policy seem particularly strong in the Central and East European context, and that we can therefore refute the view that domestic and international competition will leave no role to be played by the anti-monopoly offices.

3. Economic transformation and competition policy

Our contributors have thrown into sharp relief a number of areas in which the process of economic transformation itself brings a new and important role for competition policy. The most significant are with respect to privatisation, to the rule of law and to traditional managerial habits of collusion.

The chapters in this volume make clear that, throughout the previously socialist economies of Central and Eastern Europe, privatisation is the most important ingredient of micro-economic policy. It is being approached in quite different ways in the three countries; Poland and Czechoslovakia have in principle chosen methods of mass privatisation, though proposals have only come to fruition as yet in the CSFR. Poland initially planned to privatise using Investment Trusts as the future private owners of firms. Shares in the Trusts were to be distributed at zero prices to the population at large. However this proved to be difficult to implement for political reasons, and policy shifted to sectoral privatisation programmes. Recently, mass free privatisation has returned once more to the policy agenda. The CSFR chose a method of mass privatisation based on the free distribution of vouchers directly to the public. The first round of a complicated auction procedure for up to 1,500 firms took place during 1992. In contrast Hungary has not gone down the route of mass privatisation, relying instead on the privatisation plans of existing management or offers from other potential buyers, quite commonly from abroad, as a basis for the transfer of ownership.

These differences go some way to explain the observed variations in the role of the Competition Offices in restructuring and privatisation. The Polish Anti-Monopoly Office appears to have been best able to exploit the policy vacuum to argue in favour of restructuring and competition during the privatisation process. It is hard to evaluate their success at this early stage, but the Polish Office appears to have been very active, with examinations of hundreds of cases concerning the entire range of potential privatisations-mass commercialisations, liquidations and even attempting to restructure some of the largest firms. Mrs Fornalczyk is apologetic that her office did not put into effect a 'broad radical deconcentration policy' but the Office's achievements in this area contrast favourably with those of other countries in the region.

The Czech and Slovak governments have also been concerned to increase competition while privatising, but they would appear to have relied less on their Competition Offices as the executors of this policy. The Czech office was slow in setting up and the Slovak one has concentrated on the abuse of monopoly power. Though both have reviewed some privatisation cases, one is left with the impression that if there are pressures to restructure prior to privatisation, they are coming from elsewhere in the government apparatus.

Hungary has placed greater stress on privatisation through sale, and, as a consequence, on foreign involvement in the privatisation process. The conflict between the desire to reduce market concentration in order to improve company performance and to maintain it in order to increase the sale price is therefore more marked in the Hungarian context. Moreover, unlike in Poland, the Competition Office does not have the authority to break up existing firms prior to privatisation; ownership rights and therefore the capacity to restructure are located in the State Property Agency. Hence though the Competition Office is well established and has a forceful presence in Hungary, its impact on privatisation seems likely to be more akin to that of the CSFR's than Poland's Office.

We noted in the introduction that centrally planned economies were characterised by direct control of firms, on the basis of orders, enforced through the hierarchical structure of the Communist Party. Economic relations were in principle governed through the plan, which effectively precluded exchange between suppliers and customers. Management received orders to deliver supplies on the basis of predetermined inputs, all specified in quantitative terms. Much of the plan had the force of law, and was supported by a penal bonus system. Behind the formal plan dictates, the Communist Party stood as an hierarchy dedicated to the enforcement of central policy. Though these countries had commercial law, it had little role to play since most transactions were not voluntary. Moreover, there was little respect for the legal institutions and judiciary, which made no pretence of independence from the Communist Party.

One of the most fundamental changes required, therefore, in the transition from planning to market is the establishment and enforcement of a commercial code, and the building of faith in the independence of the judiciary. A failure to do so would bring into question the enforceability of voluntary contract, and would undermine confidence in a free market system. The Anti-Monopoly Offices in all three countries have played an important role in establishing the independence, credibility and standing of a commercial system based on the rule of law. What matters is the number of successful cases brought, and in all three countries the Competition Offices have been very active, and relatively successful in their prosecutions. It will take many years for reputations to be established, but the process will clearly be helped by a high profile of Competition Office Presidents.

However, competition policy has to be more than a symbol of the resurgence of the rule of law in commercial relations. It must also begin to affect behaviour, most notably that of managers who have survived and prospered in a system which actively opposed competitive behaviour. The new Competition Offices must begin to counteract these ingrained habits of collusion. Our contributors make clear that the magnitude of this problem is immense. For example, Polish firms responded to the initial decline in demand in January 1990 by not cutting prices, and then to the modest upturn after June by increasing prices. In the succeeding two years many have largely failed to restructure, to reorganise, to find new markets or to cut employment. Rather they have passed on rising costs resulting from falling labour productivity to consumers. Crisis cartels have been formed to manage this process, and as lobbies to raise tariffs, soften credit and increase demand. Similar enterprise responses to macro-stabilisation and price reform have been observed in Russia during 1992. We have direct experience of this problem ourselves. During a case study being undertaken by one of us in Hungary, the manager of a firm was asked why his prices were the same as those charged by his two competitors. He immediately responded that this was because there was no problems of co-ordination between them; the three managers met together monthly to agree prices!

It will take a long time to change this kind of mentality. Competition Offices have an important role to play because they can use the newly emerging force of the law to challenge existing practices, and because they can set precedents. The anti-monopoly offices in all three countries have rightly been very active in countering monopolistic practices; especially related to abuse of dominant positions. However it is notable that even in Poland, where 83 legal proceedings were started during 1991, only in 20 decisions were some alleged monopolistic practices found. One also finds a relatively low success rate from litigation in Slovakia (34 per cent of cases were abandoned and the final judgement only applied in 39 per cent). This may be intentional – the offices may be using legal proceedings as much to publicise the fight against restrictive practices as to win cases. Alternatively it could reflect a learning process in the application of the new legislation.

The authority of competition policy will be strengthened by the Association Agreements with the European Community. The potential role of anti-monopoly offices in the transition process was probably recognised by the negotiators who, for the first time in Association Agreements, explicitly included competition policy. Under the terms of the Agreements, the three economies in transition must introduce rules to prevent cartel agreements and abuse by firms of dominant positions in line with Articles 85, 86 and 92 of the Treaty of Rome after three years. As Rollo (1991) notes, the agreements give the EC considerable oversight of competition policy in the three associated states, and effectively harmonise their laws with the EC standard. Given the political significance of relations with the EC in each of these countries, the Association Agreements clearly strengthen the hand of the Competition Offices in domestic policy.

4. Models and experience of competition policy

In the Introduction, we argued that the economies in transition could choose their competition policy model 'off the shelf' (though restricted by the requirements of the Association Agreements). Areas of policy choice included judicial as against administrative systems; a focus on dominance versus market power; and public as against private enforcement.

Though there are numerous ways in which their transitional policy and experience differ, the three countries have made very similar choices in their model of competition policy. They have largely followed Central

European, and especially German, tradition in establishing a judicial policy framework, which facilitates the use of fines as penalties for infringements. The laws also follow German/EC practice in focusing upon dominance (with the definition of monopolisation involving relatively low market shares – 30–40 per cent – for such open economies) which places less emphasis on the direct promotion of competition. The bulk of anti-competitive practices also appear to be illegal on the basis of the 'rule of reason' (though our contributors are rarely explicit on this matter); they each indicate situations in which the case for defining a course of conduct as abusive has to be argued. However, though price controls remain potentially significant everywhere (the Hungarian Competition Office emerged out of the Price Office), the authorities appeared to have eschewed the use of their powers in this area, presumably because success in marketisation is seen to rely on correct price signals. Finally, the economies in transition are relying predominantly on public rather than private enforcement of competition law; in this as in most other areas, American experience is rejected in favour of European.

It would be difficult for the economies in transition to adopt an American type of competition law given the Association Agreements, and the strong political, social and economic influences from Western Europe. However, the American model seems to offer some advantages given the particular situation these countries find themselves. Given the severely imperfect market structures, it would seem attractive for competition policy to seek to extend competition itself, rather than to protect consumers directly by preventing abuse of dominant positions. Given the lack of experience (and perhaps authority) of the judiciary, clear-cut legislation which outlaws anti-competitive practices might be more suitable than 'rule of reason' cases which depend on good judgements and case law. Important steps in the same direction can however be achieved through the use of guidelines in the Competition Office. Significant private incentives to eliminate anti-competitive practices, with injured parties being able to bring civil actions against monopolists, might also help in establishing both the rule of law and in breaking down collusive practices.

There is one final subject concerning the experience of competition policy in transition. In Western countries, competition policy and the regulation of natural monopolies are kept largely if not entirely distinct. This separation is facilitated by control either being vested in the relevant ministries if the firms are nationalised, or in those of regulatory authorities if private. Competition law is rarely framed to cover the public sector. However, since most firms in the economies in transition are state-owned, public corporations have been included in the anti-monopoly legislation. This has meant that competition offices must also be responsible for the problems of natural monopolies, and their special situation is not properly recognised or even perhaps understood. For example, in Poland, the proceedings against natural monopolists were so numerous that a special team was formed to tackle them. In Slovakia, we learnt that one of the major cases in 1991 concerned the Slovak Gas corporation. An important lesson of competition policy to date is therefore that there should be special legislation to deal with natural monopolies, with the problem being removed from the scope of the anti-monopoly office, so they can then focus on markets which could in principle act in a competitive manner. Steps in this direction have recently been taken in Slovakia.

5. The role of the state in transition

This volume suggests that the establishment of Anti-Monopoly Offices operating within the framework of a West European/EC-type legislative structure has been one of the more conspicuous successes of the transition process. Such offices have a central role to play in building competitive markets, and one that complements rather than can be substituted for by international competition. Anti-monopoly legislation can have particular significance in the economies in transition in encouraging restructuring prior to privatisation, and in counteracting anti-competitive attitudes.

It is sometimes asserted that the state should have very little role in the economic transformation process. Such a perspective underlies the arguments against industrial policy and other aspects of planned economic restructuring (see e.g. Blanchard *et al.*, 1990, Lipton and Sachs, 1991, Fischer and Gelb, 1991) and has considerably more force in Central and Eastern Europe where the state apparatus is huge, incompetent and frequently corrupt, and government intervention in industry seems likely only to preserve previous structures and inefficiencies.

Competition policy, however, seems to be a measure which governments could usefully undertake in transition. Though it creates an additional layer of bureaucracy, it is devoted to enforcing new rules of the game instead of defending producers' interest; the authorities are using legislation to develop the competitive character of the market itself rather than to direct enterprise decisions towards particular output or price targets. There is an analogy here with French-type indicative planning. Many admirers saw the French planning institution in the 1950s as a motor for growth in its own right, directing investment and manipulating trade. Estrin and Holmes (1983) however argued that the planning office was too small to fulfil any operational function. Rather it used its high profile and prestige as a pressure group for growth. Its impact was most significant on management, whom it influenced in the direction of improved efficiency, and on government, whose attention was intermittently diverted from short to long-term issues.

There are parallels with competition offices in transition. The offices we have been studying do not have the authority or the expertise to restructure all the firms in their countries along the lines suggested by Newbery and Kattuman (1992). But they have prestige and a high profile, and can use their authority to argue the case for competition with firms, and within the state apparatus. For example, though these offices do not control the privatisation process, they are empowered to argue the importance of competition in each privatisation case. The enterprise sector is in a weak state during the recession, and is arguing against trade liberalisation and the loss of domestic monopoly power. These siren voices against competition, often amplified by foreign firms seeking to buy rights to future monopoly profits through privatisation, need to face an institutionalised voice within the government committed to ensuring competition as a first priority. This has emerged as the most important role currently being played by the competition offices, and one being undertaken with some degree of success.

References

Blanchard, O. *et al.*, 1990, *Reform in Eastern Europe*, Cambridge, MIT Press.

Estrin, S. and Holmes, P. M. 1983, *French Planning in Theory and Practice*, London, Allen and Unwin.

Fischer, S. and Gelb, A. 1991, 'Issues in Socialist Transition', *Journal of Economic Perspectives*, Fall.

Harberger, A. C. 1954, 'Monopoly and Resources Allocation', *American Economic Review Papers and Proceedings*, pp. 77-83.

Lipton, D. and Sachs, J. 1991, 'Creating a Market Economy in Eastern Europe', *Brookings Papers*, April.

Newbery, D. M. and Kattuman, P. 1992, 'Market Concentration and Competition in Eastern Europe', CEPR Discussion Paper no. 664.

Rollo, J. M. C. 1991 'Association Agreements Between the EC and the CSFR, Hungary and Poland. A Half Empty Glass?', Chatham House mimeo.

INDEX